Rethinking Eschatology

Rethinking Eschatology

A Postmillennial Perspective

JASON L. QUINTERN

WIPF & STOCK · Eugene, Oregon

RETHINKING ESCHATOLOGY
A Postmillennial Perspective

Copyright © 2025 Jason L. Quintern. All rights reserved. Except for brief quotations in critical publications or reviews, no part of this book may be reproduced in any manner without prior written permission from the publisher. Write: Permissions, Wipf and Stock Publishers, 199 W. 8th Ave., Suite 3, Eugene, OR 97401.

Wipf & Stock
An Imprint of Wipf and Stock Publishers
199 W. 8th Ave., Suite 3
Eugene, OR 97401

www.wipfandstock.com

PAPERBACK ISBN: 979-8-3852-3506-3
HARDCOVER ISBN: 979-8-3852-3507-0
EBOOK ISBN: 979-8-3852-3508-7

VERSION NUMBER 01/22/25

Scripture quotations are from the ESV® Bible (The Holy Bible, English Standard Version®), © 2001 by Crossway, a publishing ministry of Good News Publishers. Used by permission. All rights reserved. The ESV text may not be quoted in any publication made available to the public by a Creative Commons license. The ESV may not be translated in whole or in part into any other language.

Contents

Preface | vii

Chapter One
Introduction to Eschatology | 1

Chapter Two
Introduction to Hermeneutics | 13

Chapter Three
Old Testament Foundations | 29

Chapter Four
New Testament Foundations | 52

Chapter Five
The Olivet Discourse | 67

Chapter Six
Contextual Foundations of Revelation | 77

Chapter Seven
Interpreting Revelation | 99

Chapter Eight
Response to Common Objections | 115

Chapter Nine
Response to Specific Critiques | 129

Chapter Ten
Final Remarks | 137

Bibliography | 145

Index | 157

Preface

My journey to accepting the truth of postmillennialism began with the intriguing idea of an early date for the book of Revelation. A recommendation from a friend led me to read *Before Jerusalem Fell* by Kenneth L. Gentry Jr., a work that significantly deepened my fascination with this subject. Early influences such as Jeff Durbin, R. C. Sproul, and Douglas Wilson further shaped my understanding of Christian eschatology.

As I advanced in my formal education, my doctoral dissertation focused on defending the early date of Revelation, which inspired me to dive even deeper into the exploration of eschatological studies. This passion also motivated me to pursue other academic writings related to the subject. These activities ignited my desire to contribute more broadly to the academic field, culminating in the creation of *Rethinking Eschatology: A Postmillennial Perspective*.

One important objective of this book is to clarify key issues and dispel misconceptions surrounding postmillennialism. In chapter 8, I address common objections, drawing heavily on the works of Kenneth L. Gentry Jr. and Keith A. Mathison, who are staunch advocates of this eschatological view. Similarly, Chapter Nine dives specifically into the critiques raised by Jeremy Sexton, offering a thoughtful yet concise response to his objections.

This book is intended for theology students, pastors, and anyone with a keen interest in eschatology, particularly those seeking a clearer understanding of modern postmillennialism. While academically grounded, I have aimed to make the content accessible enough for a broader audience. My hope is that it will serve as a valuable resource for those exploring this often misunderstood perspective.

Jason L. Quintern, PhD

Chapter One

Introduction to Eschatology

ESCHATOLOGY

In Christian eschatology, there are four primary theological frameworks or systems that interpret and understand the second coming of Christ and the progression of God's kingdom. Each of these systems, namely amillennialism, premillennialism, dispensationalism, and postmillennialism, engage with the expectation of a visibly manifested return of Christ. They acknowledge key elements such as the final resurrection, divine judgment, the heavenly reward of the righteous, and the infernal punishment of the wicked. It should be emphasized, at the outset, that each of these eschatological systems rest comfortably within the broader framework of Protestant Christian orthodoxy. That is to say that each system is fully compatible with the accepted beliefs, doctrines, and teachings that characterize mainstream Protestant Christianity.[1]

While these eschatological systems agree on the final outcome—that God will ultimately triumph over sin and evil, leading to a state of eternal glory and perfection for believers—they have different views on how this belief in redemption impacts or shapes historical events. In simpler terms, they agree on the end goal but have different perspectives on how the belief in that goal affects the course of history. These differences do not result from a purposeful departure from scriptural fidelity; instead, they

---

1. Loraine Boettner observes that these systems share key presuppositions: the belief that Scripture is the authoritative word of God, the view of Christ's death as a sacrificial act satisfying divine justice and the sole basis for salvation, the expectation of Christ's future visible and personal return, the resurrection of all individuals with new bodies, the judgment before Christ's throne, the reward of the righteous in heaven, and the punishment of the wicked in hell. Boettner, *Millennium*, 3.

arise from the distinctive interpretative methodologies embraced by each theological system. The variations that occur are not due to any deliberate corruption of the Scriptures, but rather because each system employs a unique method in their interpretation.[2]

P. Andrew Sandlin rightly observes that the eschatological belief of an individual influences their evangelization efforts. A belief in the predestined catastrophe of the world may diminish motivation for evangelism, as it fosters a sense of futility. Similarly, the rejection of continuity between the Old Testament promises and the New Testament church may undermine enthusiasm and optimism.[3] It may be difficult to feel connected to Christian ministry and missions if a coherent narrative or fulfillment of God's promises is absent throughout history. Such beliefs directly impact the commitment to global evangelization, as commanded by Christ in the Great Commission (Matt 28:18–20).

The purpose of this book, therefore, is to offer a concise presentation and defense of the postmillennial view. Drawing heavily upon the works of Kenneth L. Gentry Jr. and Keith A. Mathison, considered as the primary modern advocates for this perspective, the central argument suggests that, with the empowerment of the Holy Spirit, the gospel will ultimately triumph over diverse peoples and nations. This victory is envisioned to usher in an extended period of righteousness characterized by a widespread manifestation of evangelical faith.[4] The expectation is that this transformative period will unfold before the culmination of history through the return of Christ. In other words, the postmillennial perspective is optimistic about history, asserting that the redemptive power of the gospel will progressively transform societal structures, leading to a prolonged era of righteousness and widespread adherence to Christian principles.[5]

---

2. Boettner, *Millennium*, 3.
3. Sandlin, *Postmillennial Primer*, xxvi.
4. Gentry, *Postmillennialism*, 5–6.
5. The prolonged era of peace, as depicted in the Bible, eventually gives rise to the apostasy mentioned in Rev 20. This apostasy leads to a rebellion that Christ will return to quell. For a detailed response to critiques concerning the compatibility of this sequence with postmillennialism, refer to chapter 9.

Introduction to Eschatology

DEFINING ESCHATOLOGY

In divisive theological discussions, such as the subject of eschatology, it is necessary to define key terms for comprehensibility and clarity. The use of technical vocabulary enhances precision and promotes clear communication.[6] Therefore, the first term to be defined is "eschatology," which originates from the amalgamation of two Greek words: ἔσχατος (*eschatos*), meaning "last," and λόγος (*logos*), meaning "study" or "discourse." Thus, the etymological definition of "eschatology" is understood as "the study of last things."[7] This linguistic construction finds its roots in biblical passages referring to concepts such as "the last days" (Heb 1:2), "the last hour" (1 John 2:18), and "the last time" (1 Pet 1:20), among others.[8]

Traditionally, scholars distinguish between two primary categories of eschatology: individual and general. Individual eschatology focuses on the aspects of an individual's death and the intermediate state, which refers to the period between an individual's death and their final resurrection and judgment.[9] In contrast, general eschatology is concerned with the culmination of world history and the human race. It explores the unfolding of God's kingdom throughout history, the return of Christ, the resurrection, final judgment, and the eternal state.[10] Given the nature of this study, the focus will be on this latter category.

The concept of the "millennium" originates from the first six verses of Rev 20, where it describes a thousand-year reign of Christ. The term "millennium" is derived from the Latin words *mille*, meaning "thousand," and *annum*, meaning "years," referring to this specific period mentioned in the book. Since Revelation is a highly symbolic text, interpreting this passage has led to the development of the four major eschatological frameworks, which will be defined below.

6. Riddlebarger, *Case for Amillennialism*, 27.

7. Youngblood, *Dictionary*, 369.

8. Berkhof, *Systematic Theology*, 666; Gentry, *He Shall Have Dominion*, 4; Vos, *Eschatology*, 2–3.

9. Gentry notes that the precise terminology used to categorize eschatology varies slightly amongst scholars. Gentry, for instance, employs the terms "personal" and "cosmic" eschatology. F. F. Bruce and J. J. Scott Jr. refer to these categories as "individual" and "world" eschatology. Louis Berkhof, aligning with the terminology adopted in this present work, designates them as "individual" and "general" eschatology. Gentry, *He Shall Have Dominion*, 5; Bruce and Scott, "Eschatology," in Elwell, *Evangelical Dictionary of Theology*, 386; Berkhof, *Systematic Theology*, 666.

10. Mathison, *From Age to Age*, 1–2; Erickson, *Christian Theology*, 1071.

MILLENNIAL VIEWS

As stated above, there are four major systems of eschatology that focus on the second coming of Christ: amillennialism, premillennialism, dispensationalism, and postmillennialism. This section aims to provide clarity by defining each system, briefly exploring their historical roots, and presenting contemporary theologians who support them.[11] Given the significance of the second coming of Christ in Christian doctrine, it is valuable to explore the various eschatological perspectives as they offer distinct interpretations of this event. Therefore, it becomes necessary to carefully examine each system to equip readers with a well-rounded understanding of the debate.

Amillennialism

Amillennialism emerged as a distinct eschatological system around the beginning of the twentieth century. Before this period, adherents of amillennialism identified themselves as postmillennialists, sharing the belief that Christ would return after the "millennial age."[12] They differed from postmillennialists, however, by rejecting the notion of a future earthly millennium. Amillennialists assert that the millennium passages in Rev 20, symbolize the entire period between the two advents of Christ, with the thousand years serving as a symbolic representation of the "interadvental age."[13]

Moreover, amillennialists tend to believe that Christ's kingdom will not attain global dominance. Instead, they anticipate a period of decline into apostasy prior to Christ's second coming, which will bring judgment and establish an eternal order.[14] This eschatological perspective finds its roots in the theological contributions of Augustine of Hippo (AD 354–430), whose

---

11. This section will not provide an exhaustive account of the historical roots of each system. The early church's understanding of prophecy was incomplete and rudimentary, lacking the systematic frameworks present in contemporary eschatological positions. Gentry, *He Shall Have Dominion*, 93. For a historical account of the millennium, see Wainwright, *Mysterious Apocalypse*, 21–103.

12. Riddlebarger, *Case for Amillennialism*, 39–40.

13. Kim Riddlebarger notes that the Dutch theologian Abraham Kuyper (1837–1920) is credited with being the first to use the term "amillennial." Riddlebarger, *Case for Amillennialism*, 40.

14. Cox, *Amillennialism Today*, 1–6. See also Gentry, *Postmillennialism*, 2–3; Erickson, *Christian Theology*, 1112–15.

interpretation of Revelation and focus on the spiritual nature of Christ's reign played a major role in shaping the core beliefs of both amillennialism and postmillennialism.[15] For instance, Augustine expounds on his views in his work, *The City of God*, asserting that the first resurrection mentioned in Rev 20 symbolizes the regeneration of individuals who were spiritually dead.[16] Unlike premillennialism, Augustine's teachings claim that the second resurrection occurs at the culmination of the second coming of Christ, rather than a thousand years after the first resurrection.[17]

The Reformation witnessed further development in amillennial thought, with John Calvin emerging as another contributor to the eschatological system. Calvin emphasized Christ's present spiritual reign while also rejecting the concept of a literal millennium. Mathison, however, points out that Calvin supported a key element of later postmillennialism, specifically expressing confidence in the conversion of a significant majority of humanity to Christ before the second coming.[18] In contemporary discussions, theologians such as Sam Storms and Cornelis P. Venema have continued to articulate and defend the amillennial perspective.[19]

Premillennialism

Premillennialism, also known as "historic premillennialism" to distinguish itself from dispensational premillennialism, teaches that Christ will return visibly to the earth to establish a literal thousand-year reign before the final judgment. This view holds that the current phase of God's kingdom involves the gathering of the elect into the church, followed by a future descent into the great tribulation. During this period, there will be the rise of the antichrist, widespread apostasy in the church, and significant global turmoil. Christ's return will culminate in the final resurrection, the battle of Armageddon, and the establishment of a literal one-thousand-year reign marked by righteousness and peace on earth. The millennium concludes

---

15. Gentry argues that Augustine's optimistic views are closely aligned with that of postmillennialism. Gentry, *He Shall Have Dominion*, 101–4.

16. Augustine, *City of God*, 20.6.

17. Mathison, *Postmillennialism*, 29–30; Wainwright, *Mysterious Apocalypse*, 36–39.

18. Mathison, *Postmillennialism*, 39. See also Holwerda, *Exploring the Heritage*, 110–39; Calvin, *Institutes*, 3.20.42.

19. Storms, *Kingdom Come*, 549–59; Venema, *Promise of the Future*, xvii. See also Ridderbos, *Coming of the Kingdom*.

with the release of Satan, a rebellion, divine intervention, the final resurrection, the judgment of all mankind, and the establishment of the eternal state.[20]

In the early church, prominent figures such as Justin Martyr (ca. AD 100–165) and Irenaeus (ca. AD 120–202) expressed a literal interpretation of the millennium, picturing it as a period characterized by abundance, fertility, and the renewal of the earth. Millard J. Erickson notes that this period, often referred to as *chiliasm*, was characterized by a distinct focus on sensory appeal and the construction of a glorified Jerusalem. This perspective faced opposition from figures such as Clement of Alexandria (ca. AD 150–215), Origen (ca. AD 195–253), and Dionysius (ca. AD 200–265). The decline of *chiliasm* can be attributed in part to Augustine's alternative view of the millennium, as discussed above.[21]

During the Middle Ages, this eschatological view became scarce. It experienced a revival in the nineteenth century, largely attributed to John Nelson Darby, who played a key role with the introduction of dispensational premillennialism.[22] This eschatological system, which emphasizes distinct periods in God's plan for humanity, will be discussed in greater detail below. However, Craig L. Blomberg, Sung Wook Chung, and George Eldon Ladd provide modern interpretations of historic premillennialism.[23]

Dispensationalism

Dispensationalism is a variant of premillennialism that emerged in the nineteenth century, particularly through the teachings of Darby, an influential

---

20. Ladd, *Gospel of the Kingdom*, 16–23. See also Mathison, *Postmillennialism*, 9; Gentry, *Postmillennialism*, 3; Erickson, *Christian Theology*, 1109–12; Storms, *Kingdom Come*, 135–37.

21. Erickson, *Christian Theology*, 1110; Visser, "Ancient Christian Eschatology," 10–11, 15–17, 21; Wainwright, *Mysterious Apocalypse*, 21–30. For information on Irenaeus's view of *chiliasm*, see Hill, *Regnum Caelorum*, 254–59.

22. One of the main differences between historic premillennialism and dispensational premillennialism lies in their view of the relationship between Israel and the church: historic premillennialism sees the church as the spiritual continuation and fulfillment of Israel, while dispensational premillennialism maintains a distinct separation between Israel and the church. Dispensationalism views Israel as having distinct promises, purposes, and a future national and spiritual restoration separate from the church. Grenz, *Millennial Maze*, 128–31.

23. Blomberg and Chung, *Case for Historic Premillennialism*; Ladd, *Gospel of the Kingdom*, 16–23.

figure in the Plymouth Brethren movement.[24] This eschatological system divides history into seven dispensations or eras, each representing a distinct way in which God interacts with humanity. Darby's teachings gained traction, and dispensationalism became widely disseminated, notably through the Scofield Reference Bible in the early twentieth century.[25]

According to this eschatological system, the present "Church Age"[26] will end with rapture, marking the beginning of a seven-year great tribulation on the earth. This tribulation concludes with the battle of Armageddon, where Christ returns to defeat his enemies. The nations are then judged, with supporters of Israel entering Christ's millennial kingdom, while others face judgment. Christ rules from Jerusalem, the temple is rebuilt, and animal sacrifices are reinstated as memorials (this last point is disputed among dispensationalists).[27] After the millennium, Satan leads a rebellion before being crushed by divine intervention. The wicked then face judgment, leading to the commencement of the eternal state.[28] Contemporary teachings of dispensationalism can be found in the works of Charles Caldwell Ryrie, John F. Walvoord, and John MacArthur.[29]

---

24. Around 1826, John Nelson Darby, a clergyman of the Anglican Church of Ireland, was ordained in Wicklow but resigned in 1827. He joined the "Brethren" sect, founded by A. N. Groves, rejecting traditional church practices. Internal conflicts caused schisms in Plymouth (1845) and Bristol (1847). Darby led the stricter faction, forming the "Darbyites." He toured and preached in various countries from 1830 until his death in 1882. Darby developed his eschatological system in response to his postmillennial teachers at Trinity College in Dublin. Thus, dispensationalism was created as an anti-postmillennial system. Cross and Livingstone, *Oxford Dictionary*, 376; Bass, *Backgrounds to Dispensationalism*, 64–140; Sweetnam and Gribben, "Darby and the Irish Origins," 575–76; Sandlin, *Postmillennial Primer*, 2; Wainwright, *Mysterious Apocalypse*, 82.

25. Dispensationalists use the term "rapture" to describe the church's union with Christ during his second coming. The term originates from the Latin *rapio*, meaning "caught up." The key biblical passage supporting this concept is 1 Thess 4:15–17. However, interpretations differ on how the timing of the rapture relates to the tribulation period marking the end of the age. Robert G. Clouse, "Rapture of the Church," in Elwell, *Evangelical Dictionary of Theology*, 983. For a discussion regarding when dispensationalists place the rapture, see Archer et al., *Three Views on the Rapture*.

26. The term "Church Age" is commonly used in dispensational theology to describe the period between Pentecost and the Rapture. Walvoord, *Prophecy*, 374, 384.

27. For more information, see Mathison, *From Age to Age*, 254–56.

28. Ryrie, *Basis of the Premillennial Faith*, 155–57; Campbell and Townsend, *Coming Millennial Kingdom*, 270–71; Mathison, *Postmillennialism*, 9; Gentry, *He Shall Have Dominion*, 360–64; Gentry, *Postmillennialism*, 4–5; Wainwright, *Mysterious Apocalypse*, 81–86.

29. Ryrie, *Dispensationalism Today*; Walvoord, *Millennial Kingdom*; MacArthur,

Rethinking Eschatology

Objections to Dispensationalism

Dispensationalism, like historic premillennialism, asserts that Christ will return before a literal thousand-year reign on the earth, involving separate physical resurrections for the converted and unconverted.[30] However, this view can be refuted by demonstrating that Christ is currently reigning from heaven, the first resurrection in Rev 20:5–6 refers to spiritual regeneration, and Paul's teaching negates the idea of separate resurrections for believers and unbelievers. This section will briefly address these points to challenge the dispensational premillennial interpretation.[31]

First, the New Testament clearly affirms that Christ is presently reigning from heaven. Acts 2:32–36 describes how Christ was exalted to the right hand of God, where he now reigns as Lord until all of his enemies are made a footstool for his feet (cf. Ps 110:1). Ephesians 1:20–22 further emphasizes that Christ is seated at God's right hand, far above all rule and authority. This present reign contradicts the premillennial notion that Christ's kingdom is yet to come in a future, earthly form.

Second, Rev 20:4–6 refers to the "first resurrection," which premillennialists interpret as a physical resurrection occurring before the millennium. However, a more consistent interpretation is that this "first resurrection" symbolizes spiritual regeneration—the believer's new birth and resurrection with Christ (cf. John 5:24–25; 11:25–26; Eph 2:1–6; Col 3:1–4).[32] This interpretation aligns with the rest of Scripture, which speaks of a spiritual resurrection through faith in Christ as the first experience of new life, in contrast to the final physical resurrection of all mankind at the end of the age.

Third, Paul, in 1 Cor 15:22–24, explicitly states that the resurrection of the dead occurs at Christ's second coming, followed immediately by "the end" when he delivers the kingdom to God the Father *after* having abolished all rule, authority, and power: "For as in Adam all die, so also in Christ shall all be made alive. But each in his own order: Christ the firstfruits, then at his coming those who belong to Christ. Then comes the end, when he delivers the kingdom to God the Father after destroying every rule

---

Essential Christian Doctrine.

30. George Eldon Ladd, "Historic Premillennialism," and Herman A. Hoyt, "Dispensational Premillennialism," in Clouse, *Meaning of the Millennium*, 17–40; 63–92.

31. For a comprehensive critique of dispensationalism, see Gerstner, *Wrongly Dividing the Word of Truth*.

32. Sandlin, *Postmillennial Primer*, 23–24.

and every authority and power." This sequence leaves no room for a literal thousand-year interlude between the resurrection of the righteous and the final judgment. If "the end" comes at Christ's return, as Paul asserts, then the notion of a subsequent earthly millennium is unscriptural.[33]

Therefore, the dispensational view is inconsistent with the New Testament's teaching on Christ's current reign, the nature of the first resurrection, and the timing of the end. A proper interpretation of the relevant passages points instead to Christ's ongoing spiritual reign, the current experience of spiritual resurrection by believers, and a unified resurrection and final judgment at the second advent.

Postmillennialism

Postmillennialism is an optimistic eschatological system that envisions a millennial period within history preceding the second coming of Christ. Similar to amillennialism, many adherents of this position interpret the "thousand years" mentioned in Rev 20 symbolically, understanding it as an extended period before Christ's return. According to this interpretation, there will be a "golden age" for the church during which the gospel, empowered by the Holy Spirit, will draw the majority of humanity to Christ. The key difference between these views is that postmillennialists expect the millennium to result from the church's active influence through the spread of the gospel, while amillennialists see the millennium as the present Church Age, with no expectation of a global Christian transformation before Christ's return.

Postmillennialists assert that Christ established his kingdom spiritually through the church in the first century, during his first advent, initiating a progressive growth of Christianity that would eventually lead to the global dominance of righteousness and prosperity. The millennium culminates with Christ's return, a general resurrection, final judgment, and the establishment of the eternal order. As the Church Age concludes, Satan will be unleashed for a final rebellion against the kingdom of God. However, this rebellion will be swiftly defeated with the return of Christ, marking the ultimate triumph of righteousness.[34]

---

33. Sandlin, *Postmillennial Primer*, 24.

34. Bloesch, *Essentials*, 192–95; Wilson, *Commentary*, 229–41; Boettner, *Millennium*, 4; Erickson, *Christian Theology*, 1107–9; Gentry, *Postmillennialism*, 5–6; Mathison, *Postmillennialism*, 10; Wainwright, *Mysterious Apocalypse*, 77–81.

Elements of postmillennial optimism can be found in the writings of the early church fathers and the Reformers.³⁵ Historically, the eschatological view of prominent Reformers initially followed an Augustinian perspective.³⁶ This perspective persisted through the Puritan era, where, like their predecessors, the Puritans employed a historicist interpretation of Revelation, considering it a prophecy outlining the historical trajectory of the church. However, the Puritans expanded upon the hopeful prophecies in Scripture, which led to them embracing a distinctively optimistic eschatology.³⁷

Figures such as Thomas Brightman (1562-1607), John Cotton (1584-1652), Thomas Goodwin (1600-1679), and Philipp Jakob Spener (1635-1705) in the sixteenth and seventeenth centuries, along with Daniel Whitby (1638-1726) in the eighteenth century, articulated postmillennial perspectives.³⁸ Their outlook anticipated the conversion of Jews and expected positive transformations within the church. The eighteenth century witnessed a surge in the popularity of postmillennialism, with advocates such as John Guyse (1680-1761), Philip Doddridge (1702-1751), and Thomas Scott (1747-1821) advocating for this perspective in England.³⁹ In

---

35. Erickson argues that characteristics of each of the millennial systems can be found throughout the church history. Erickson, *Christian Theology*, 1107. For a more detailed examination of the historical roots of postmillennialism, see Gentry, *He Shall Have Dominion*, 90–111.

36. Martin Luther, like Augustine, rejected *chiliasm* and interpreted Rev 20 as describing the ongoing existence of the church. He saw eschatological events, including the presence of the antichrist linked to the papacy, unfolding in the present. Luther believed that the antichrist's presence signaled the imminent end times, asserting that the millennium was fulfilled in early church history. His eschatological perspective was marked by urgency and hope, anticipating the near-future occurrence of the final judgment and Christ's return. Althaus, *Theology of Martin Luther*, 410–25. See also Mathison, *Postmillennialism*, 38.

37. Mathison notes John Owen's anticipation of unprecedented gospel success. He states that Owen identified six divine promises for the present age: peace for the gospel and its followers, purity in ordinances and worship, widespread conversions, elimination of will worship, global submission to Christ, and triumphant overcoming of opposition. Mathison, *Postmillennialism*, 42. For more information regarding Puritan eschatology, see Beeke and Jones, *Puritan Theology*, 773–88; Murray, *Puritan Hope*, 221–32; Bloesch, *Essentials*, 193.

38. Cotton, *Churches Resurrection*, 19–21, 30; Whitby, "Treatise of the True Millennium," 2:251–78; Goodwin, *Works of Thomas Goodwin*, 72; Zakai, *Exile and Kingdom*, 46–55; Bloesch, *Essentials*, 193; Grenz, *Millennial Maze*, 68–69; Mathison, *Postmillennialism*, 41–45; Murray, *Puritan Hope*, 46–47; Wainwright, *Mysterious Apocalypse*, 78.

39. Guyse, *Practical Expositor*, 351–60; Doddridge, *Family Expositor*, 492–98; Scott,

America, influential proponents like Jonathan Edwards (1703-1758) and Samuel Hopkins (1721-1803) envisioned the millennium as a direct result of the church's agency, something that would come about through the active involvement or influence of the church itself.[40]

While traditional postmillennialists anticipated the millennium unfolding in the future, others, like David Hartley (1705-1757), believed that it commenced with the first advent of Christ. Hartley suggested that, before Christ's return, the gospel would reach all nations through the missionary efforts of the church, and the Jews would return to Palestine.[41] Frederick Denison Maurice (1805-1872) similarly integrated a belief in church progress with the Augustinian view of the millennium, asserting that the millennial kingdom commenced with Christ's first advent.[42]

Although postmillennialism witnessed a decline in popularity during the twentieth century, there has been a recent resurgence of interest in this system.[43] Within contemporary discussions, proponents of postmillennialism, including Keith A. Mathison, Douglas Wilson, and Kenneth L. Gentry Jr., remain active in articulating and defending this perspective.[44] Since each of these eschatological systems stem from the "millennium" mentioned in Rev 20, the following chapter will provide an overview of various hermeneutical methods and interpretive approaches to understanding the book of Revelation.

Holy Bible, 964-67; Wainwright, *Mysterious Apocalypse*, 79.

40. Edwards, *Works of Jonathan Edwards*, 609-11; Hopkins, "Treatise on the Millennium," 5-8; Gentry, "Postmillennialism" in Bock, *Three Views on the Millennium*, 17; Mathison, *Postmillennialism*, 45; Wainwright, *Mysterious Apocalypse*, 79.

41. Hartley, *Observations on Man*, 373-80; Wainwright, *Mysterious Apocalypse*, 80.

42. Maurice, *Lectures on the Apocalypse*, 376-401; Wainwright, *Mysterious Apocalypse*, 81.

43. The diminishing prevalence of postmillennialism as the predominant eschatological perspective has been attributed to a convergence of factors, notably the aftermath of two world wars, the influence of liberal theology on religious institutions, and the secularization of the Western world. Lightner, *Last Days Handbook*, 110-11. See also Moorhead, "Erosion of Postmillennialism," 61-77; Quandt, "Religion and Social Thought," 390-409.

44. Wilson, *Heaven Misplaced*; Gentry, *He Shall Have Dominion*; Mathison, *Postmillennialism*. See also Bahnsen, *Victory in Jesus*; Davis, *Christ's Victorious Kingdom*; Rushdoony, "Postmillennialism Versus Impotent Religion," 122-27.

SUMMARY

This introductory chapter explored the various systems within Christian eschatology, focusing on the second coming of Christ and the trajectory of God's kingdom. It has presented the four major eschatological positions: amillennialism, premillennialism, dispensationalism, and postmillennialism. Each system shares fundamental beliefs such as the final resurrection, divine judgment, and the eternal state but diverges in interpretations of how these events unfold in history. Historical roots of postmillennialism trace back to figures like Augustine and the Puritans who envisioned a hopeful future for the church. While support for postmillennialism declined in the twentieth century, contemporary proponents, such as R. C. Sproul, Greg L. Bahnsen, Douglas Wilson, James R. White, Keith A. Mathison, and Kenneth L. Gentry Jr., have revived interest in the system.

Chapter Two

Introduction to Hermeneutics

HERMENEUTICS

Hermeneutics is a specialized field of study dedicated to theory and methods of interpretation. It places a particular emphasis on understanding how the texts convey meaning and examines the cognitive processes involved in interpreting these texts.[1] In essence, hermeneutics explores how one makes sense of and derives meaning from ancient and biblical documents. In this context, "meaning" refers to the message the author intentionally put into the text for the benefit of the original audience.[2] Walter C. Kaiser Jr. and Moisés Silva explore the multifaceted nature of the term "meaning," highlighting its components: a referent (the subject discussed), a sense (the message conveyed about the referent), an intention (the author's communicated purpose through language), and its significance (the connection between meaning and external elements such as individuals, ideas, or contexts).[3]

Jacob Élisée Cellérier defines hermeneutics as "the science that teaches the principles of interpretation," with a particular focus on biblical hermeneutics, which determines how to interpret the holy Scriptures.[4] This

---

1. Brown, *Introducing Biblical Hermeneutics*, 20; Schökel, *Manual of Hermeneutics*, 19.

2. Goldsworthy, *Gospel-Centered Hermeneutics*, 27.

3. Kaiser and Silva also point out additional definitions, including the concept of value, which represents preferences or priorities. They illustrate this with the example of a particular book of the Bible holding more "meaning" for an individual compared to other books. Kaiser and Silva, *Introduction to Biblical Hermeneutics*, 35–46.

4. Cellérier, *Biblical Hermeneutics*, 3.

field acknowledges the diversity of human thought and the potential for ambiguities in expression. Its primary goal is to bridge any perceived gaps between authors and readers, ensuring that the true and accurate meaning intended by the writer is grasped by the audience.

Milton S. Terry (drawing from Cellérier) distinguishes between "general" and "special" hermeneutics. General hermeneutics deals with principles applicable to the interpretation of all languages and writings, incorporating the logical operations of the human mind and the philosophy of human speech. In contrast, special hermeneutics focuses on interpreting specific books and types of writings, such as historical, poetical, philosophical, and prophetic texts, each requiring distinct principles and methods suited to its unique characteristics and style.[5] Special hermeneutics is described as a practical and almost empirical science, focused on finding rules and solutions for interpretation. In contrast, general hermeneutics is characterized as methodical and philosophical, seeking overarching principles and methods.[6]

Hermeneutics holds an important role among theological sciences, especially for conservative Protestant Christians who view the Bible as *sola scriptura* (Scripture alone), not merely *prima scriptura* (primarily Scripture).[7] According to the Reformers' perspective, the Bible stands as the sole authoritative voice of God to humanity. In contrast, the Roman Catholic Church and the Eastern Orthodox Church recognize the Bible as a primary authority alongside other sources such as ancient creeds, decisions of ecumenical councils, and oral traditions that are considered as equally important.[8] Thus, for Protestants, an accurate interpretation of Scripture is crucial to effectively grasp God's message, as it stands as the sole authoritative and infallible guide for their faith and practice.[9]

Specifically, for the focus of this present work, a targeted hermeneutical approach to the book of Revelation will be established. With approximately four hundred direct quotations or allusions to the Old Testament, Revelation stands as the most Hebraic book in the New Testament.[10]

---

5. Terry, *Biblical Hermeneutics*, 17–20.
6. Cellérier, *Biblical Hermeneutics*, 3.
7. Ramm, *Protestant Biblical Interpretation*, 1.
8. Ramm, *Protestant Biblical Interpretation*, 1.
9. For more information regarding the authority and infallibility of Scripture, see White, *Scripture Alone*.
10. For more information related to the Hebraic nature of Revelation, see Gentry,

Therefore, this author argues that the grammatical-historical method provides the most accurate framework for interpreting the Apocalypse of John. This method involves analyzing the text's grammar, syntax, and historical setting to uncover its meaning as intended in its original context.

OVERVIEW OF HERMENEUTICAL METHODS

This section examines various hermeneutical methods, offering a brief overview of other common interpretive methods. While this is by no means an exhaustive presentation of hermeneutical methods, this overview will set the stage for a detailed analysis of why the grammatical-historical approach is particularly suited for interpreting the book of Revelation. This section, therefore, aims to equip readers with a well-rounded understanding of foundational interpretive methods in biblical scholarship.

Allegorical Method

In the early church, the dominant method of biblical interpretation was allegorical, meaning that texts were read with the belief that they contained deeper, spiritual meanings beyond their literal sense. Allegorical interpretation involves viewing a text on two levels: its literal surface meaning and a deeper spiritual significance.[11] This method prevailed until the late Middle Ages despite occasional criticisms from early church fathers like Jerome and Augustine who argued it sometimes disregarded the text's literal meaning. In contrast, the Antiochene School advocated for a more literal and historical approach, emphasizing understanding within its historical context and maintaining fidelity to the text's literal sense. Despite these critiques and the Antiochene preference for literalism, allegorical interpretation remained widely practiced.[12]

Divorce of Israel, 1:153–56. See also Ford, *Revelation*, 27.

11. For instance, the Israelites crossing the Red Sea was seen not only a historical event but also as a symbol of Christ's redemption. Law, *Historical-Critical Method*, 27. See also Robert B. Sloan Jr. and Carey C. Newman, "Ancient Jewish Hermeneutics," in Corley et al., *Biblical Hermeneutics*, 61–63.

12. Law, *Historical-Critical Method*, 28–32.

Proof-Text Method

The proof-text method is characterized by its practical and pastoral focus, aiming to find biblical passages that support specific themes or pastoral positions, frequently through selective citation. It often relies on isolated verses or phrases without considering their original context or the author's intended meaning. This approach can lead to misinterpretations by treating scriptures as standalone statements rather than coherent parts of a larger narrative or theological framework. Some argue that this method overlooks the historical and literary context of the texts, potentially distorting their original message and authority.[13]

Historical-Critical Method

The historical-critical method involves detailed analysis of biblical texts to uncover their literary sources, historical contexts, and cultural settings. It seeks to understand texts through rigorous scholarly methods, such as source criticism, textual criticism, and historical analysis.[14] This approach prioritizes understanding how ancient texts were composed and received, often focusing on the text's historical meaning over its normative or theological implications for contemporary readers. It could be said that while this method is valuable for academic study, it may diminish the text's coherence and relevance for modern faith and practice.[15]

Reader-Response Method

The reader-response method emphasizes the role of the reader in interpreting biblical texts, allowing individuals to determine the text's meaning based on their personal responses and contexts. It acknowledges the importance of historical and critical analysis but highlights the diversity of interpretations that emerge from different readers' perspectives. This approach is criticized for potentially diminishing the authority of the text

---

13. Kaiser and Silva, *Biblical Hermeneutics*, 33.

14. In the context of biblical interpretation, "criticism" denotes the scholarly examination of literary texts concerning aspects such as their origins, textual formation, composition, content analysis, and historical context. Hernando, *Dictionary of Hermeneutics*, 17.

15. Kaiser and Silva, *Biblical Hermeneutics*, 33–34.

by prioritizing subjective reader interpretations over the author's original intent and the text's historical context. This may also undermine the text's unity and authoritative meaning.[16]

Grammatical-Historical Method

The grammatical-historical method focuses on understanding biblical texts by closely examining their linguistic features and historical contexts. It seeks to uncover the author's intended meaning as understood by the original audience, emphasizing the significance of grammar, syntax, and cultural background.[17] This method interprets passages within their literary units (pericopes) to grasp their theological relevance both in their original historical context and for contemporary application.[18] This approach preserves the authority of the biblical texts by grounding interpretations in rigorous linguistic and historical analysis, thereby maintaining fidelity to the text's original message and theological content.[19]

DEVELOPMENT OF INTERPRETATION

This present work will now explore the development of biblical interpretation, providing a concise overview of influential ideas and scholars that have shaped this field across history. While not exhaustive, understanding this progression is useful for contextualizing contemporary hermeneutical methods and appreciating the diverse approaches that have shaped modern scholarship. By doing so, this author argues that readers will gain a comprehensive understanding of the historical backdrop of interpretation, thereby enhancing their appreciation of the complexity of biblical exegesis throughout the centuries.

---

16. Kaiser and Silva, *Biblical Hermeneutics*, 34.
17. Hernando, *Dictionary of Hermeneutics*, 83–84.
18. Kaiser and Silva, *Biblical Hermeneutics*, 34.
19. The historical-critical method analyzes the origins, sources, and historical context of biblical texts, often with a naturalistic and skeptical perspective. In contrast, the grammatical-historical method focuses on understanding the original meaning intended by the author through linguistic and historical analysis, typically affirming traditional interpretations and the divine inspiration of the text.

Reformation (Sixteenth Century)

Martin Luther emphasized that the Bible stood as the ultimate authority in theological matters, superior to any ecclesiastical jurisdiction. He largely dismissed allegorical interpretations, except for when they directly concerned Christ rather than the papacy. Luther insisted that the original revelation of God could only be fully apprehended through diligent study of the Hebrew and Greek scriptures. Interpreters were urged to consider grammar, historical context, and the specific circumstances surrounding biblical authors. Luther affirmed that any knowledgeable Christian possessed the capability to interpret Scripture, emphasizing its inherent clarity in conveying its message to believers.[20]

John Calvin approached the biblical text through the lens of his classical humanist training, thoroughly analyzing its grammatical and rhetorical features in the original languages and historical context. Calvin's method involved initially reading the text in Hebrew or Greek, followed by translating it into Latin, often providing explanations for his chosen Latin renderings.[21] Similar to Luther, Calvin opposed allegorical interpretation, which he believed obscured the true meaning of Scripture. He stressed the importance of grammatical exegesis, linguistics, contextual analysis, and the principle of comparing scriptures that address similar subjects ("Scripture interprets Scripture").[22]

Post-Reformation (Seventeenth to Eighteenth Centuries)

According to Ramm, the post-Reformation era was marked by theological severity, with a strong emphasis on doctrinal purity often leading to "heresy hunting" and strict adherence to established Protestant creeds. In response to this environment, Pietism emerged as a movement seeking to reclaim the Bible for spiritual nourishment and personal edification. Philipp Jakob Spener, a key figure in Pietism, viewed the Bible as God's instrument for fostering genuine spirituality.[23]

August Hermann Francke, influenced by Spener, became a notable advocate of Pietistic biblical interpretation. Francke emphasized interpreting

---

20. Ramm, *Protestant Biblical Interpretation*, 53–55.
21. Yarchin, *History of Biblical Interpretation*, 184.
22. Ramm, *Protestant Biblical Interpretation*, 58–59.
23. Ramm, *Protestant Biblical Interpretation*, 60–61.

each Scripture passage within the broader context of Christ's person and work. Gerald Bray highlights Francke's insistence on grammatical-historical exegesis as crucial for deepening one's understanding of the text, leading naturally to a holier lifestyle.[24]

In contrast, John Owen, educated at the University of Oxford and steeped in the intellectual culture of Western Europe, emphasized the centrality of Scripture. According to Carl R. Trueman, Owen stressed the necessity of biblical language proficiency, arguing that without it theological commitment to Scripture's authority would be practically undermined. Owen believed ministers and theologians should possess a profound grasp of Hebrew, Greek, and the cultures from which these languages emerged.[25]

Jonathan Edwards drew his perspective on the Bible from the Protestant Reformation, emphasizing its power, sufficiency, and authority. Like the Reformers, he valued the literal sense of Scripture while also exploring its spiritual depths. Although he recognized the importance of grammatical, historical, and cultural contexts, he cautioned against relying solely on these for a "speculative knowledge" of divinity. Edwards believed true spiritual understanding of Scripture, accessible only to the "Spirit-filled," transcends mere intellectual knowledge, leading to genuine acceptance of God's word.[26]

Modern Era (Nineteenth to Twentieth Centuries)

Louis Berkhof traces the development of biblical interpretation through various schools. Johann August Ernesti founded the grammatical school, advocating for the literal sense of Scripture, disapproving of allegorical interpretations except where explicitly indicated by the original author. He emphasized treating the Bible grammatically like any other book.[27] The historical school, initiated by Johann Salomo Semler, highlighted the human, historical origin of Scripture, suggesting that many parts of the Bible

---

24. Bray, *Biblical Interpretation*, 241–42.

25. Carl R. Trueman, "John Owen as a Theologian," in Oliver, *John Owen*, 44–48.

26. Stein, "Quest for the Spiritual Sense," 101, 106–7, 108–9.

27. Berkhof, *Principles of Biblical Interpretation*, 33. For a detailed discussion of the development of "modern exegesis," see Farrar, *History of Interpretation*, 397–487. See also Virkler, *Hermeneutics*, 69–73.

were shaped by their historical context and were not necessarily meant to be universally applicable.[28]

David Friedrich Strauss, influenced by Georg W. F. Hegel, proposed a mythical interpretation, viewing the messianic idea as evolving historically. Ferdinand Christian Bauer, of the Tübingen school, applied Hegelian principles to argue that New Testament texts emerged from theological conflicts.[29] Friedrich Schleiermacher, associated with the mediating school, marginalized biblical inspiration, treating the Bible as akin to secular texts. Immanuel Kant emphasized a moral interpretation of Scripture, asserting its value in promoting ethical improvement.[30]

Within the realms of Christian Protestantism, B. B. Warfield, reflecting on Charles Hodge as an exegete and teacher, critiques Hodge's approach.[31] He suggests that although Hodge presented multiple viewpoints on grammatical and lexical issues, his decisions often lacked a strong linguistic foundation and occasionally reflected personal or theological biases rather than sharp critical judgment. This occasionally led to misapplications of texts in supporting unrelated doctrines. However, Hodge's strength, remarks Warfield, lay in his ability to "grasp" and articulate the overall meaning of passages, a skill "few men could equal."[32]

According to Andreas J. Köstenberger, Adolf Schlatter stressed the importance of distinguishing between historical exegesis and dogmatics.[33] He believed that New Testament theology, as a historical discipline, should come before any systematic presentation of Scripture. Schlatter insisted that historical research should strictly rely on available sources and avoid speculative source-critical questions. He viewed Jesus' teachings through the lens of his actions, highlighting that Jesus' main goal was to establish God's saving reign rather than to provide doctrinal or ethical instruction.[34]

---

28. Berkhof, *Principles of Biblical Interpretation*, 33–34.

29. Berkhof, *Principles of Biblical Interpretation*, 35.

30. Berkhof, *Principles of Biblical Interpretation*, 36.

31. B. B. Warfield's discussion of Charles Hodge was presented in the form of a letter addressed to Hodge's sons, A. A. Hodge and C. W. Hodge. Meeter, *Selected Shorter Writings*, 437–40.

32. Meeter, *Selected Shorter Writings*, 439.

33. Andreas J. Köstenberger, "Preface: The Reception of Schlatter's New Testament Theology 1909-23," in Schlatter, *Theology of the Apostles*, 10–11.

34. Andreas J. Köstenberger, "Preface: The Reception of Schlatter's New Testament Theology 1909-23," in Schlatter, *Theology of the Apostles*, 10–11.

William W. Klein, Craig L. Blomberg, and Robert L. Hubbard Jr. trace the development of interpretation through the two world wars. They highlight that World War I marked a pivotal moment, shattering the optimism of liberal theology. Karl Barth emerged as a prominent critic of liberalism, advocating for the authority of Scripture and emphasizing personal encounters with God.[35] Meanwhile, Rudolf Bultmann, influenced by Martin Heidegger's existentialism, applied form criticism to the Gospels. He questioned their historical reliability and sought to "demythologize" the Bible, attempting to make its message pertinent to modern audiences. Bultmann's existentialist approach required a subjective reading of Scripture, focusing on its existential relevance rather than its historical accuracy.[36]

Klein, Blomberg, and Hubbard note that World War II further shaped biblical interpretation, giving rise to the biblical theology movement in America. This movement emphasized the Bible's theological coherence and its relevance to contemporary life. Redaction criticism emerged, focusing on the theological intentions of biblical authors. Bultmann's students initiated the "new quest for the historical Jesus," attempting to harmonize historical research with faith.[37] The "new hermeneutic" that followed stressed the dynamic interaction between the text and the reader, influencing the reader-response approach to biblical interpretation. Later developments in the late twentieth century included "Pentecostal hermeneutics" and the "Third Quest for the Historical Jesus," which explored new archaeological and manuscript evidence to understand Jesus within his historical context.[38]

OVERVIEW OF CRITICISMS

Just as hermeneutical methods are distinguished between general and special; criticisms are also classified as either higher criticism or lower criticism.

---

35. Klein et al., *Introduction to Biblical Interpretation*, 104. For more information about Karl Barth's perspective on the historical Jesus and the relationship between the historical-critical method and dogmatic theology, see Weber, "Karl Barth and the Historical Jesus," 350–54.

36. Klein et al., *Introduction to Biblical Interpretation*, 105.

37. Klein et al., *Introduction to Biblical Interpretation*, 106–7.

38. Klein et al., *Introduction to Biblical Interpretation*, 108–10. The "quest" for the "historical Jesus" refers to the effort to understand the historical figure of Jesus of Nazareth apart from theological interpretations. This endeavor seeks to reconstruct the life of Jesus using historical methods. Albert Schweitzer's book examines the lives of previous scholars and their research related to this topic. Schweitzer, *Quest of the Historical Jesus*.

Higher criticism involves analyzing the forms and sources of biblical texts using scientific and literary critical tools. It focuses on understanding the origins, authorship, and historical context of the texts. Lower criticism, on the other hand, aims to establish the most accurate version of the biblical manuscripts and texts.[39] Thus, this section aims to equip readers with a well-rounded understanding of common criticism approaches in biblical scholarship.

Historical Criticism

Historical criticism, or higher criticism, seeks to uncover the historical context in which a text was written, encompassing its cultural, social, and political setting, along with significant historical events that may have shaped the text. According to James D. Hernando, it aims to explain the historical and literary details that describe a text's composition, addressing aspects such as authorship, date of composition, intended audience, sources, authenticity, historical purpose, literary unity, genre, and style. Its objective includes constructing a chronological narrative that reconstructs relevant events and explores their interconnections whenever possible.[40]

Source Criticism

Source criticism identifies and analyzes the sources authors used to compile texts, such as the Pentateuch. Julius Wellhausen suggests these texts evolved from various documents reflecting Israel's religious development. Hernando states that this approach recognizes that biblical authors used written sources, which is supported by explicit statements (Num 21:14; Luke 1:1) and internal evidence like parallels in Gospel accounts. Source critics examine how authors combined these sources, focusing on literary development to reveal theological insights about the author or originating communities.[41]

---

39. McKim, *Westminster Dictionary*, 128.
40. Hernando, *Dictionary of Hermeneutics*, 71–72.
41. Hernando, *Dictionary of Hermeneutics*, 76–77.

Form Criticism

Form criticism involves studying and categorizing the literary patterns and typical features of texts to uncover the contexts that shaped them. It examines various literary forms and genres like parables, hymns, and miracle stories, aiming to trace back to their original oral traditions and understand their function in their original settings.[42] Bultmann argues that since Aristotle's time, traditional hermeneutic rules have guided the interpretation of literary texts, emphasizing formal analysis of a work's structure and style. Effective interpretation involves analyzing the composition, understanding each element in relation to the whole, and grasping both the parts from the whole and the whole from its individual elements.[43]

Redaction Criticism

Redaction criticism examines how biblical writers edited their source material, analyzing how editors (redactors) shaped and structured sources to convey specific theological or ideological messages. In other words, it focuses on the editorial process and intent behind the editing. Mark Goodacre emphasizes that historical studies of the Synoptic Gospels often involve an analysis to uncover unique redactional elements that offer insights into the writers' perspectives and their communities.[44]

INTERPRETIVE APPROACHES TO REVELATION

In the analysis of the book of Revelation, scholars and theologians have traditionally employed four basic interpretative approaches: historicism, idealism, futurism, and preterism.[45] These perspectives provide distinct

---

42. James D. G. Dunn, "Form Criticism," in Gooder, *Searching for Meaning*, 21–23.

43. Bultmann, *Essays*, 235–36. For more information on the impact of form criticism, see Muilenburg, "Form Criticism and Beyond," 1–18.

44. Mark Goodacre, "Redaction Criticism," in Gooder, *Searching for Meaning*, 38–40.

45. In recent discussions, an emerging method called eclecticism has gained attention. This approach seeks to integrate two or more existing approaches into a unified method of interpretation. Essentially, eclecticism can be seen as a modified version of idealism, although it is not commonly regarded as a basic approach. For more information on the eclectic approach, see Osborne, *Baker Exegetical Commentary*, 21. For a critique of this method from a dispensational perspective, see Thomas, *Revelation 1–7*, 32–35.

insights into the prophetic text, presenting varied frameworks for comprehending its meaning. This section will examine the specific attributes of each interpretative approach, explaining the key features associated with each method.[46]

Historicism

Historicism is the interpretive method that views the text of Revelation as a pre-written historical narrative. This narrative is believed to span from the time of the author to the ultimate culmination of the world.[47] In essence, historicism sees Revelation as a prophecy unfolding through time, detailing God's overarching plan for history. This approach views Revelation as serving as a predictive account of church history, commencing with the first advent of Christ and extending towards the anticipated second coming, marking significant milestones in the progression of the Christian church.[48]

Idealism

Idealism sees Revelation as symbolizing timeless principles, not specific historical events.[49] In other words, it suggests that Revelation represents enduring truths rather than detailing specific historical occurrences. Robert H. Mounce notes, "Its proponents hold that Revelation is not to be taken in reference to any specific events but as an expression of those basic principles on which God acts throughout history."[50] Thus, idealism focuses on

---

46. The various approaches to the book of Revelation have also been briefly discussed in the present author's doctoral dissertation, from which much of this information is derived. Quintern, "Neronic Date," 6–7.

47. Gregg, *Revelation*, 13.

48. Arthur W. Wainwright attributes the historicist approach to Joachim of Fiore's (ca. 1135–1202) teachings, while Mathison highlights its adoption by Protestant Reformers, pointing out its limited adherence in contemporary times. Stanley J. Grenz also notes that the historicist view was held by the early church and many of the Reformers. Wainwright, *Mysterious Apocalypse*, 49–53; Mathison, *From Age to Age*, 648; Grenz, *Millennial Maze*, 178–79. For more information regarding historicism, see Gentry, *Navigating*, 32–34. For an interpretation of Revelation from the historicist approach, see Lee, *John's Revelation Unveiled*.

49. Smalley, *Thunder and Love*, 146.

50. Mounce, *Book of Revelation*, 28.

the spiritual aspects of historical events, avoiding a direct examination of the historical characters and events themselves.[51]

Futurism

Futurism posits that all the prophesied occurrences from Rev 4:1 onwards are yet to take place. Futurists, in other words, interpret the events as being future, transpiring shortly before the second coming of Christ. Mathison, a preterist, notes, "This conclusion grows out of a belief that there is no correspondence between these prophesied events and anything that has yet occurred in history."[52] The main idea behind the futurist perspective is that the majority of the prophetic events described in the book of Revelation are anticipated to occur in the future, typically with a literal fulfillment.[53]

Preterism

Preterism interprets the prophecies in the book of Revelation as events that were future for the original author but are now in the past. According to this perspective, these prophecies were mostly fulfilled in the first century with the destruction of Jerusalem and the Second Temple.[54] Gentry observes that elements of this perspective can be identified in certain early church fathers like Irenaeus (ca. AD 120–202) and Hippolytus (ca. AD 170–236). However, it gains significant prominence at a later period when the Jesuit Luis De Alcazar formalizes and systematizes it in the early seventeenth century.[55] The author of this present work employs the partial-preterist ap-

---

51. For information regarding idealism's strengths and weaknesses, see Gentry, *Navigating*, 34–36. For an interpretation of Revelation from the idealist approach, see Minear, *I Saw a New Earth*.

52. Mathison, *From Age to Age*, 648.

53. Gentry observes that futurism has been embraced by Christians since the early 1900s. After a period of obscurity from the fifth century, it experienced a revival in the sixteenth century, spearheaded by Francisco Ribera (1537–1591), a Spanish Jesuit scholar. In modern times, futurism has become prominent in America, notably due to the influence of dispensationalism. Gentry, *Navigating*, 36–38; Smalley, *Thunder and Love*, 146. For an interpretation of Revelation from a futurist perspective, see Walvoord, *Revelation of Jesus Christ*.

54. Gregg, *Revelation*, 13.

55. The Society of Jesus, more commonly known as the Jesuits, is a society within the Roman Catholic Church that was founded by Ignatius of Loyola (1491–1556) and

proach as his interpretive method when analyzing the book of Revelation. The following section will discuss the differences between partial-preterism and full-preterism.

Comments Regarding Full-Preterism

As this present study contends that Revelation's symbolic events are representative of the destruction of Jerusalem and the Second Temple, it is important to offer a brief discussion of the preterist interpretive framework adopted within this book.[56] Storms notes that some proponents of an extreme preterist interpretive approach, often referred to as hyper- or full-preterism, assert that the second coming of Christ occurred in AD 70. According to their view, this second coming constituted a judgment against Israel, leading to the destruction of Jerusalem and the Second Temple, but it did not involve a visible return of Jesus to the earth. They contend that this event also encompassed the fulfillment of the final resurrection, final judgment, and the establishment of the new heavens and new earth.[57] Partial-preterism, by contrast, views these final prophecies as future events.

Sandlin contends that the theological stance of full-preterism undermines orthodox Christianity by rejecting the future visible and physical return of Christ, the resurrection of the righteous and unrighteous, and the final judgment—all of which are asserted by major Reformation confessions, including those of the Anglican, Baptist, Lutheran, and Presbyterian traditions.[58] According to Sandlin, the denial of these fundamental biblical tenets aligns full-preterism with historical groups such as the ancient gnostics and "anti-supernaturalistic" liberals, marking a departure from the doctrinal consensus established by mainstream Protestant Christianity.[59]

---

instituted by Pope Paul III in 1540. The order was established in response to the need for reform within the church and as part of the Counter-Reformation, which sought to respond to the Protestant Reformation. For more information on the early Jesuits, see MacCulloch, *Reformation*, 212–19. Gentry, *Navigating*, 38.

56. This section has been adapted from the present author's dissertation. Quintern, "Neronic Date," 7–8.

57. Storms, *Kingdom Come*, 261–62.

58. Sandlin, *Postmillennial Primer*, 55–56.

59. Sandlin, *Postmillennial Primer*, 56.

Scholars widely recognize J. Stuart Russell as an influential advocate for the full-preterist position.[60] In summarizing this approach, Russell articulates it as follows:

> We conclude, therefore, that all the parts of our Lord's prediction refer to the same period and the same event; that the whole prophecy is one and indivisible, resting upon the same foundation of divine authority. Further, that all that was cognisable by the human senses is proved to have been fulfilled, and, therefore, we are not only warranted, but bound to assume the fulfillment of the remainder as not only credible, but certain. . . . We are compelled, therefore, by all these considerations, and chiefly by regard for the authority of Him whose word cannot be broken, to conclude that the Parousia, or second coming of Christ, with its connected and concomitant events, did take place, according to the Saviour's own prediction, at the period when Jerusalem was destroyed, and before the passing away of "that generation."[61]

Mathison has provided a thorough critique of full-preterism, characterizing it as a heretical belief system situated outside the boundaries of "orthodox Christianity."[62] He notes that traditional Christian eschatology has consistently encompassed the belief in the "future visible coming of Jesus" for the universal judgment of humanity and the "future bodily resurrection" of all individuals. In light of their rejection of these theological doctrines, full-preterists have effectively positioned themselves outside the theological framework of historic Christianity and are accordingly regarded as holding heretical beliefs.[63]

SUMMARY

This chapter has explored hermeneutics, the study of interpretation, emphasizing its importance in understanding ancient and biblical texts. Key scholars, such as Walter C. Kaiser Jr., Moisés Silva, and Jacob Élisée Cellérier, highlight the components and principles of meaning, distinguishing

---

60. Sandlin, *Postmillennial Primer*, 57; Hillegonds, *Early Date of Revelation*, 199–201; Sproul, *Last Days*, 79–101; Mathison, *Postmillennialism*, 235.

61. Russell, *Parousia*, 548–49. For another full-preterist work, see King, *Cross and the Parousia*.

62. Mathison, *Postmillennialism*, 244. For a thorough critique of full-preterism, see Mathison, *When Shall These Things Be?*

63. Mathison, *Postmillennialism*, 244.

between general and special hermeneutics. The chapter highlighted the role of hermeneutics in theology, particularly for conservative Protestants adhering to *sola scriptura*, and advocates for the grammatical-historical method for interpreting the book of Revelation, given its numerous Old Testament references.

The chapter traces the historical development of biblical interpretation from the Reformation to the modern era, providing context for contemporary methods. It also presents four interpretive approaches to the book of Revelation: historicism, idealism, futurism, and preterism. The rest of the book will present the case for postmillennialism, the optimistic eschatological view that the gospel will triumph globally before Christ's return, leading to an era of righteousness and widespread evangelicalism.

Chapter Three

Old Testament Foundations

OLD TESTAMENT

This chapter focuses on exploring the portrayal of the Messiah's reign over an expansive earthly kingdom as depicted in the Psalms and the Prophets within the Old Testament. While recognizing the potential for extensive discussion on the postmillennial hope found in the Pentateuch and the historical books, this section's attention is directed towards the optimism articulated within these specific texts.[1] In essence, the Old Testament prophecies about the Messiah's reign often include optimistic visions of a future where all nations will ultimately come to worship God. Through exegetical analysis and careful examination of select passages, this chapter aims to contribute to a deeper understanding of God's redemptive plan and the ultimate destiny of creation as envisioned in the Psalms and the Prophets.

The Psalms

Psalm 2

> Why do the nations rage and the peoples plot in vain? The kings of the earth set themselves, and the rulers take counsel together, against the LORD and against his Anointed, saying, "Let us burst their bonds apart and cast away their cords from us." (Ps 2:1–3)

---

1. For a comprehensive examination of biblical eschatology from a postmillennial perspective, see Gentry, *He Shall Have Dominion*; Mathison, *From Age to Age*.

Setting the tone for the entire psalm, verse 1 raises a rhetorical question, highlighting the futility of human opposition against God's chosen king. The Hebrew phrase "his anointed" (מָשִׁיחַ) refers to the Messiah, signifying the chosen or appointed one of God, typically associated with kingship or leadership. In Ps 2, it denotes the king whom God has selected to rule over his people. This prophetic passage anticipates the reign of Jesus Christ as God's appointed king (cf. Acts 4:25–26; 13:32–33; Heb 1:5).[2] The "nations" and "peoples" represent humanity's rebellion against divine authority.[3] Matthew Poole suggests that "nations" refers to the gentiles who opposed both David (2 Sam 5:6, 17; 1 Chr 14:8) and Christ (Luke 18:32; Acts 4:25). He also suggests that "peoples" could either refer to the same group or to the Israelites who similarly opposed David (2 Sam 2:8) and Christ (Acts 4:27).[4]

Verse 2 shifts the focus to the united efforts of earthly rulers as they oppose both God and his Messiah. Joseph A. Alexander notes that the shared target of attack here—the Anointed One and God—indicates their intimate relationship. In Acts 4:25–27, this description is applied to Herod, Pilate, Jews, and gentiles against Jesus Christ, representing the ultimate fulfillment of the prophecy. This clarifies that "nations" does not solely refer to gentiles but rather to entire communities opposing divine authority, distinct from individual resistance.[5]

Verse 3 reflects the rebellious sentiment of the nations, expressing their longing to break away from God's authority and the rule of his appointed king. Their desire for independence leads them to rebel against divine governance, yet their defiance is destined to end in failure. John Gill observes that these words are spoken by the kings and rulers of the earth who aim to discard the laws, ordinances, and truths of Jesus Christ. The verse denotes their lack of reverence for God, their rejection of Christ and his teachings, their refusal to submit to him, and their disdain for his gospel and commandments. Gill adds that those who seek to reject Christ envision freedom in breaking away from him, yet they end up enslaved to their own desires and sinful pleasures, becoming servants of corruption (cf. Rom 6:16).[6]

---

2. Brown et al., *Lexicon*, 603.

3. The term "nations" (גּוֹי, *goy*) typically refers to gentile nations or non-Israelite peoples. Brown et al., *Lexicon*, 156.

4. Poole, *Commentary*, 2:2.

5. Alexander, *Psalms*, 21–22.

6. Gill, *Exposition*, 496.

> He who sits in the heavens laughs; the Lord holds them in derision. Then he will speak to them in his wrath, and terrify them in his fury, saying, "As for me, I have set my King on Zion, my holy hill." (Ps 2:4–6)

This verse depicts an image of God's reaction to the rebellion of the nations and their leaders. Rather than showing fear or concern, God responds with amusement and mockery. This imagery communicates God's absolute sovereignty and highlights the insignificance of human opposition in his sight (cf. Ps 37:13; 59:8; Prov 1:26–27; Isa 40:22–23). Poole draws attention to the contrast between the divine authority of "He who sits in the heavens" and the earthly reign of kings. This serves as evidence of God's clear understanding and unwavering power over all earthly affairs. Furthermore, Poole emphasizes that God's laughter signifies his disdain and mockery towards human rebellion, exposing it as futile and foolish in his eyes (cf. 2 Kgs 19:21; Ps 37:13).[7]

In verse 5, the tone shifts from laughter to divine judgment. Despite God's initial response of amusement, he will ultimately respond with righteous anger and judgment against the rebellious nations. The imagery of divine speech and fury highlights the seriousness of their rebellion and the consequences they will face. Some note that the dramatic imagery emphasizes the cosmic significance of God's declaration of his king in Zion, instilling terror in earthly rulers.[8]

Verse 6 marks a decisive declaration of God's sovereignty and the establishment of his Messiah's authority. Despite the opposition of the nations, God affirms his choice of king and asserts his reign from Zion, the holy hill representing his presence and authority. Zion (צִיּוֹן), also known as the "holy hill" of God, holds symbolic significance throughout the Old Testament as the dwelling place of God's presence and the seat of his kingship (cf. Ps 48:1–2; Isa 2:2–4). In Ps 2:6, God declares, "I have set my King on Zion, my holy hill," highlighting the divine origin and authority of the Messiah's reign (see Heb 12:22).[9]

Gentry suggests a connection between Ps 2 and Exod 15. In Exod 15, Moses' celebration song commemorates God's triumph over Egypt during the Exodus and foresees the impending terror of Israel's adversaries, the Canaanites. Similarly, Ps 2 depicts Christ's ultimate victory over the

---

7. Poole, *Commentary*, 2:2–3.
8. Craigie and Tate, *Psalms 1–50*, 66.
9. Brown et al., *Lexicon*, 851. See also Youngblood, *Dictionary*, 1217–18.

tumultuous nations of the world, mirroring God's triumph over Israel's historical enemies in the Old Testament.[10]

> I will tell of the decree: The LORD said to me, "You are my Son; today I have begotten you. Ask of me, and I will make the nations your heritage, and the ends of the earth your possession. You shall break them with a rod of iron and dash them in pieces like a potter's vessel." (Ps 2:7–9)

In verse 7, the phrase "today I have begotten you" signifies the Messiah's coronation or ascension to the throne. Alexander explains that this phrase essentially means "I am your father," echoing 2 Sam 7:14's contrast of "I will be to him a father, and he shall be to me a son." Had it been "today I am your father," it would *not* imply that the relationship started on that day but rather a formal recognition at that moment.[11] Alexander concludes that Heb 5:5 quotes Ps 2:7 to demonstrate Christ's authority came by the Father's recognition of him as son. This recognition was reaffirmed at Christ's baptism and transfiguration (Matt 3:17; 17:5).[12]

In verse 8 of Ps 2, God grants the Messiah authority and dominion over the nations. Christ is invited to make requests of God, who promises to grant him the nations as his inheritance and the ends of the earth as his possession. Gill notes that the terms "nations" and "ends of the earth" symbolize God's elect people among the gentiles, living in distant regions. These individuals are regarded by Christ as part of his flock, given to him by the Father (cf. John 6:37; 10:12). Christ's dominion is not limited to Zion or the Jewish chosen ones; rather, it extends to the gentiles as well (Isa 49:6; Rom 10:12; Eph 2:13–14). These gentiles are valued by Christ as his inheritance, signifying their inclusion in the New Testament and the expansive extent of Christ's kingdom, which encompasses the entire earth.[13]

Verse 9 depicts the Messiah's exercise of authority and judgment over the rebellious nations.[14] Robert Jamieson, A. R. Fausset, and David Brown assert that any heathen nation that refuses to acknowledge Christ as their

---

10. Gentry, *Postmillennialism*, 17.
11. Alexander, *Psalms*, 24.
12. Alexander, *Psalms*, 25.
13. Gill, *Exposition*, 498.
14. In the ancient Near East, the scepter symbolized kingship, while iron represented strength. Egyptian rulers, depicted as early as the Narmer Palette (ca. 3200–3000 BC), are shown wielding a rod or scepter in battle against their enemies. Walton et al., *IVP Bible Background Commentary*, 519.

Old Testament Foundations

rightful ruler will face his authority, depicted symbolically here as a scepter of iron, symbolizing the crushing defeat of anti-Christian opposition (cf. Matt 21:44).[15] The phrase "dash them in pieces like a potter's vessel" implies effortless destruction, possibly denoting insignificance in the object. This portrayal of the Messiah as a harbinger of destruction aligns with New Testament teachings (Rom 9:22–23; 2 Thess 1:8–9; Rev 19:15).[16] It emphasizes the heightened punishment awaiting those who reject Christ, with Christ himself as the agent of destruction for the non-elect (cf. Luke 19:27).

> Now therefore, O kings, be wise; be warned, O rulers of the earth. Serve the LORD with fear, and rejoice with trembling. Kiss the Son, lest he be angry, and you perish in the way, for his wrath is quickly kindled. Blessed are all who take refuge in him. (Ps 2:10–12)

The psalmist addresses the rulers of the earth, advising them to exercise wisdom and heed the warning given. In verse 11, the psalmist instructs the rulers to serve the Lord with reverence and awe. The expression "rejoice with trembling" signifies the combination of joy and extreme reverence for God's authority.[17]

Verse 12 contains a warning and a promise of blessing. The rulers are urged to "kiss the Son," symbolizing their submission and adoration to the Messiah (cf. 1 Sam 10:1; 1 Kgs 19:18; Hos 13:2). Rabbi Solomon B. Freehof contends that the phrase "kiss the Son" is inaccurately translated due to the ambiguity of the word בַּר (*bar*), which means "son" in Aramaic but "purity" in Hebrew. Thus, he proposes that the correct interpretation of the text should be "do homage in purity."[18]

Regardless of either translation, the essential point remains unchanged: failure to bow down to the Messiah will result in divine judgment, as indicated by the warning of his anger and swift wrath. However, there is also the promise of blessing for those who take refuge in him, highlighting the hope of salvation and protection for those who submit to the king's authority. Poole notes that "blessed are all who take refuge in him" applies

---

15. Jamieson, Fausset, and Brown also reference the prophecy in Daniel about the kingdom represented by a great mountain that emerges from a stone and shatters the image representing various kingdoms, particularly the iron kingdom (Dan 2:34–35, 44). This prophecy signifies the eventual triumph of Christ's kingdom, which will endure eternally, destroying all opposition. Jamieson et al., *Commentary*, 2:1:107–8.
16. Alexander, *Psalms*, 25.
17. Goldingay, *Psalms*, 102.
18. Freehof, *Book of Psalms*, 15.

only to Christ and cannot apply to David, who always dissuades mankind from putting their trust in princes or in any person or thing other than God (Pss 20:7; 44:6; 62:6–8; 118:8; 146:3).[19]

Overall, Ps 2 reveals God's absolute sovereignty over nations and his certain triumph over their rebellion (2:1–6). It emphasizes Jesus Christ as God's appointed ruler, whose kingdom expands universally to include Jews and gentiles (2:7–8). The imagery of Christ's coronation symbolizes his authority over all the earth (2:6). The psalm foresees the gospel's irresistible advance, shattering opposition and leading to the fulfillment of God's promises (2:9–12). This gradual triumph unfolds over time as the gospel transforms individuals and societies, ultimately bringing all Christ's enemies under his dominion (1 Cor 15:24–28; cf. Ps 110).

Psalm 22

> My God, my God, why have you forsaken me? Why are you so far from saving me, from the words of my groaning? O my God, I cry by day, but you do not answer, and by night, but I find no rest. (Ps 22:1–2)

Psalm 22:1–2, prophetically anticipates Christ's cry on the cross (Matt 27:46), portraying his full identification with humanity's suffering and his bearing of the penalty for sin through penal substitution (Isa 53:5–6; Rom 3:23–26; 2 Cor 5:21; Gal 3:13; 1 Pet 2:24). John Calvin asserts that Christ experienced the sensation of being forsaken by his Father, as he was not exempt from the fear that God's judgment instills in sinners.[20] Peter's testimony in Acts 2:24 confirms that Christ did not escape the pains of death entirely, given his representation of humanity and assumption of our sins.

Thus, Calvin notes, it was necessary for him to face God's judgment as our sin bearer. This led to the dread that compelled him to pray for deliverance from death, not because departing from life was unbearable, but because he faced God's curse.[21] Christ's cry on the cross indicates that Ps 22, while expressing David's distress, was prophetically composed concerning Christ.[22]

---

19. Poole, *Commentary*, 2:4.
20. Calvin, *Psalms*, 361.
21. Calvin, *Psalms*, 361.
22. David Dickson compares the sufferings of David to those of Christ, identifying

For the sake of brevity, attention is now directed to verses 27–28, which directly articulate the postmillennial anticipation of Christ's reign:

> All the ends of the earth shall remember and turn to the LORD, and all the families of the nations shall worship before you. For kingship belongs to the LORD, and he rules over the nations. (Ps 22:27–28)

Psalm 22 paints a vivid picture of a future global recognition of God's sovereignty, where all the elect from every corner of the earth will turn to him in repentance and worship. Poole identifies the phrase "all the ends of the earth" as referring to all nations, prophesying their inclusion in the knowledge of God and Christ through the gospel.[23]

Moreover, the passage emphasizes that all authority and kingship ultimately belong to God, and he governs the nations according to his divine purposes. Alexander observes that God's dominion extends beyond the Jews to encompass the gentiles and all nations. While his kingdom was initially established in Israel, he intends to expand it globally, establishing his throne and governance throughout the world (cf. Pss 96:10; 97:1; 99:1; Obad 21; Zech 14:9; Rom 3:29–30).[24]

Psalm 110

> The LORD says to my Lord: "Sit at my right hand, until I make your enemies your footstool." The LORD sends forth from Zion your mighty scepter. Rule in the midst of your enemies! Your people will offer themselves freely on the day of your power, in holy garments; from the womb of the morning, the dew of your youth will

---

four commonalities and differences. In this comparison, both David and Christ experience: (1) a sense of wrath, (2) temptation to doubt and desperation, (3) wrestling against temptation and trouble, and (4) ultimately achieving victory. However, they differ in: (1) the magnitude of their troubles, with Christ's being greater, (2) the nature of their troubles, as David's was probatory while Christ's was punishment due to bearing the sins of humanity, (3) the sinlessness of their temptation, with David's being tainted by sinful imperfections while Christ's was entirely sinless, and (4) the source of their strength in wrestling and victory, with David relying on Christ's strength while Christ prevails in his own strength, unified with the strength of the Father. Dickson, *Commentary on the Psalms*, 106–7.

23. Poole, *Commentary*, 2:36.

24. Alexander, *Psalms*, 113–14.

be yours. The LORD has sworn and will not change his mind, "You are a priest forever after the order of Melchizedek." (Ps 110:1–4)

Psalm 110 is the most quoted or alluded to Old Testament text in the New Testament (Matt 22:44; 26:64; Mark 12:36; 14:62; 16:19; Luke 20:41–44; 22:69; Acts 2:33–35; 1 Cor 15:25; Eph 1:20; Col 3:1; Heb 1:3, 13; 5:6; 7:17, 21; 10:12–13; 12:2).[25] In the first century, the Jews interpreted Ps 110 as prophesying the advent of the Messiah, characterized by his lineage from the royal house of David. Jesus, however, pointed out to his contemporaries that the messianic figure transcends mere familial ties to David, as evidenced by David's own acknowledgment of the Messiah as his superior, denoted by the honorific title "my Lord."[26]

The first "LORD" (יהוה, *Yahweh*) refers to God the Father, who speaks to the second "Lord" (אדני, *Adonai*) which indicates the divinity of the Messiah. Alexander points out that the figure described as superior and sovereign over David cannot be David himself or any of his descendants except Jesus. Jesus, by virtue of his dual nature (Rom 1:3–4), is both the sovereign and son of David. Alexander notes that this identification of the Lord with the Messiah was widely accepted among ancient Jews, evident from their traditions. Furthermore, Christ himself used this interpretation to argue for the Messiah's divine nature. His opponents, unable to refute this, remained silent (Matt 22:46).[27]

The command for the Lord to "sit at my right hand" denotes a position of honor, authority, and power (cf. Gen 48:14–20; Exod 15:6; Isa 41:10). Matthew Henry explains that the depiction of Christ seated at the right hand of God signifies both his exalted status and sovereign rule, symbolizing the honor bestowed upon him and the responsibilities entrusted to him by the Father.[28] Henry notes that every blessing bestowed upon humanity by God and every act of worship offered by humanity to God are mediated through Christ (1 Tim 2:5).[29] His present position at the right hand of the Father, as affirmed in various biblical passages (Mark 16:19; Acts 2:33; Rom 8:34; Col 3:1; Heb 10:12), signifies the ongoing expansion and reign of his kingdom throughout history.

---

25. Mathison, *Postmillennialism*, 80.

26. Purkiser, "Psalms," 373; Kidner, *Psalms 73–150*, 428. See also Mathison, *Postmillennialism*, 80.

27. Alexander, *Psalms*, 464–65.

28. Henry, *Commentary*, 3:659.

29. Henry, *Commentary*, 3:659.

The phrase "until I make your enemies your footstool" emphasizes the inevitability of Christ's victory. It speaks to the progressive conquest of his enemies throughout history, as his kingdom advances and prevails over all opposition. Jacob Marcellus Kik observes that the apostle Peter, on the day of Pentecost, references Ps 110:1, affirming that Pentecost fulfills this prophecy (Acts 2:34–35). Peter does not interpret this as a singular cataclysmic event reserved for the day of judgment; rather, "He sees its fulfillment in the outpouring of the Holy Spirit upon the church."[30]

In verse 2, the phrase "The LORD sends forth from Zion your mighty scepter" portrays Christ as the divine king whose dominion extends over all the earth. Henry asserts that the Messiah, upon assuming his position at the right hand of the Father, establishes a church on the earth where he reigns as king on the holy hill of Zion (Ps 2:6), in contrast to Mount Sinai where the law was given (Heb 12:18, 24). The scepter or rod symbolizes his eternal gospel, empowered by the Holy Spirit (Isa 53:1; Rom 1:16). Henry argues that through the proclamation of this gospel and the accompanying power of the Spirit, mankind will be brought into obedience to God and governed according to his will.[31]

Verse 3 of the text illustrates the theme of obedience and unwavering allegiance among Christ's followers. Mathison interprets this verse as a poetic depiction of Christ leading a "dedicated volunteer army into battle."[32] Verse 4 attributes to the messianic figure an enduring priesthood modeled after the archetype of Melchizedek (Gen 14:18–20). The biblical account of Melchizedek highlights the combination of kingship and priesthood, eagerly awaited in the anticipated messiah. Poole observes that Christ holds the dual roles of king and priest eternally, with no successor and with no end (Heb 7:3).[33]

The Prophets

Isaiah 2

> The word that Isaiah the son of Amoz saw concerning Judah and Jerusalem. It shall come to pass in the latter days that the mountain

---

30. Kik, *Eschatology of Victory*, 24.
31. Henry, *Commentary*, 3:659.
32. Mathison, *Postmillennialism*, 81.
33. Poole, *Commentary*, 2:173.

> of the house of the Lord shall be established as the highest of the mountains, and shall be lifted up above the hills; and all the nations shall flow to it, and many peoples shall come, and say: "Come, let us go up to the mountain of the Lord, to the house of the God of Jacob, that he may teach us his ways and that we may walk in his paths." For out of Zion shall go forth the law, and the word of the Lord from Jerusalem. He shall judge between the nations, and shall decide disputes for many peoples; and they shall beat their swords into plowshares, and their spears into pruning hooks; nation shall not lift up sword against nation, neither shall they learn war anymore. (Isa 2:1–4)

The verses in Isa 2:1–4 bear a striking resemblance to those in Mic 4:1–3 which has sparked debate about their origin.[34] Some theories suggest accidental displacement or scribal errors, others suggest that the texts had shared sources, or that both received direct inspiration from the Holy Spirit.[35] Regardless, the phrase "in the latter days" is pertinent to the study at hand. This term points to a future era, further explained in the New Testament, where Peter, in Acts 2:16–17, connects Christ's exaltation with the beginning of the eschatological "last days."[36]

Gentry discusses the concept of the "last days" or "latter days" as mentioned in both the Old and New Testaments, particularly in relation to the arrival of the Messiah, Jesus Christ. He suggests that the prophetic references in the Old Testament pointing towards the end times began with Christ's first coming, marking the beginning of the "last days" era.[37] This era is characterized by the establishment of Christ's kingdom, initially through the church and the new covenant initiated by Jesus (Acts 2:16–21; Heb 1:2; 9:26; 12:18–17; 1 Pet 1:20; cf. Isa 2:2; 24:23; 32:15; 37:32; Zech 12:10; Joel 2:32; Obad 1:17, 21; Mic 4:7). Thus, the "last days" are seen as beginning with Christ's first coming, with the church serving as the central point of his kingdom, and they continue into the present day.[38]

If the "last days" commenced in the first century, it becomes important to discern Isaiah's depiction of these times. In Isaiah's vision, the "mountain of the house of the Lord" serves as a symbol of God's ultimate authority and sovereignty, destined to surpass all other powers and command

---

34. For a thorough comparison of Isa 2:1–4 and Mic 4:1–3, see Watts, *Isaiah 1–33*, 45.
35. Alexander, *Isaiah*, 36–37.
36. Mathison, *Postmillennialism*, 84.
37. Gentry, *He Shall Have Dominion*, 326.
38. Gentry, *He Shall Have Dominion*, 326–27.

reverence from all nations. This imagery signifies the establishment of God's kingdom as the supreme authority over all earthly dominions. T. K. Cheyne highlights the contrast between this mountain and Sinai, where earlier revelations were bestowed in a more "limited" manner. Mount Zion, according to Isaiah, is envisioned as the eventual epicenter of "religious unity" for the entire world.[39]

Isaiah further elaborates on how the nations will respond to this kingdom. He describes how "all the nations" and "many peoples" will express a longing to ascend to the mountain of the Lord, seeking instruction and guidance in his ways. Calvin observes that this vision entails a restraint of all forms of sin, with everyone, regardless of status, being obligated to adhere to the rule of obedience by staying within the boundaries set by the word of God.[40] The imagery of turning weapons of war into tools for agriculture symbolizes the establishment of lasting peace and prosperity.[41]

Mathison points out that Isaiah's portrayal of the "last days" implies that there are events yet to transpire in the preset era, surpassing "anything we have experienced so far."[42] He contends that Isa 2 sees the fulfillment of the assurances made to Abraham regarding the blessing of all nations through the worship of the true God (Gen 12:3; 18:8; 22:18), noting that the cessation of warfare in Isaiah's vision signifies the remarkable extent of this conversion.[43] Ultimately, the Great Commission (Matt 28:19–20) will be successful as "history will experience widespread faith in God, righteousness on the personal and social levels, and international peace and prosperity on the cultural and political levels."[44] This vision of a harmonious and just world inspires hope and commitment to the ongoing work of spreading the gospel to all the nations.

Isaiah 9

> For to us a child is born, to us a son is given; and the government shall be upon his shoulder, and his name shall be called Wonderful Counselor, Mighty God, Everlasting Father, Prince of Peace. Of

---

39. Cheyne, *Prophecies of Isaiah*, 15.
40. Calvin, *Isaiah*, 96.
41. Motyer, *Isaiah*, 52.
42. Mathison, *Postmillennialism*, 85.
43. Mathison, *Postmillennialism*, 99.
44. Gentry, *Postmillennialism*, 20.

the increase of his government and of peace there will be no end, on the throne of David and over his kingdom, to establish it and to uphold it with justice and with righteousness from this time forth and forevermore. The zeal of the LORD of hosts will do this. (Isa 9:6–7)

The conquest of the Northern tribes by Tiglath-Pileser III in 733 BC led to their subjugation and the occupation of the Galilean region (2 Kgs 15:29). Previously, these tribes had supported Jeroboam over David's dynasty (1 Kgs 12:1–20). Walter Elwell notes that, despite their suffering under foreign rule, there persisted a belief in a future deliverance that was tied to the lineage they had once rejected.[45] This belief laid the groundwork for the concept of the messiah, a figure eagerly awaited, especially in times of political turmoil like the post-exilic period. The expectation of a messianic savior promised redemption and restoration, becoming a central theme in Jewish theological thinking.[46]

The passage above expands on the prophecies concerning the coming of a divine figure named Immanuel (Isa 7:14). It highlights how this figure, identified as Jesus in the New Testament, is described with divine titles such as "Wonderful Counselor, Mighty God, Everlasting Father, Prince of Peace," suggesting his divine nature.[47] In Acts 2:29–35, Peter speaks about the fulfillment of the Davidic promise in Jesus during Pentecost. He emphasizes that Jesus not only fulfills the expectations placed on the lineage of David but that he has also ascended to the right hand of God, surpassing even David in stature and authority.[48]

Alexander notes parallels between Isa 9:6–7 and Mic 5:2–4, highlighting the promise of a Davidic king bringing peace, righteousness, and uniting Israel.[49] This promise extends to the gentiles, with "peace" encompassing both the absence of war and the continual increase of power and prosperity. The king's lineage emphasizes fulfillment of promises to David (2 Sam 7:11–16; 23:1–5; 1 Kgs 8:25). Hence, the Messiah is not only called the son of David, but David himself, symbolizing a restoration or continuation of David's reign (Jer 30:9; Ezek 34:23, 24; 37:24; Hos 3:5).[50]

45. Elwell, *Commentary*, 482.
46. Herbert, *Isaiah 1–39*, 74.
47. Mathison, *Postmillennialism*, 85.
48. Gentry, *Postmillennialism*, 18–19.
49. Alexander, *Isaiah*, 134–35.
50. Alexander, *Isaiah*, 135.

The essence of Isaiah's prophecy about the reign of Christ is that it envisions a future where peace, justice, and righteousness prevail under his rule. This prophecy suggests that Christ's kingdom will gradually expand, bringing prosperity to all those within. The kingdom is not expected to be a sudden catastrophic event; rather, the growth of his kingdom is expected to "increase" progressively.[51] The certainty in this prophecy arises from divine inspiration, with the assurance of its realization emphasized by God's committed "zeal" (קִנְאַת, *qin'at*) to bring it to fruition.[52]

Isaiah 11

> They shall not hurt or destroy in all my holy mountain; for the earth shall be full of the knowledge of the LORD as the waters cover the sea. In that day the root of Jesse, who shall stand as a signal for the peoples—of him shall the nations inquire, and his resting place shall be glorious. In that day the Lord will extend his hand yet a second time to recover the remnant that remains of his people, from Assyria, from Egypt, from Pathros, from Cush, from Elam, from Shinar, from Hamath, and from the coastlands of the sea. He will raise a signal for the nations and will assemble the banished of Israel, and gather the dispersed of Judah from the four corners of the earth. (Isa 11:9–12)

Isaiah 11 presents a prophecy anticipating the arrival of the Messiah, symbolically referred to as the "Branch" (נֵצֶר, *netser*) or the "shoot from the stump of Jesse," signifying lineage from David (11:1).[53] Just as David was uniquely chosen from Jesse's family to receive great honor, a future figure from the same lineage is foretold to emerge (cf. 1 Sam 16:1–3; 2 Sam 7:18).[54] This awaited Messiah will be filled with the Spirit of the Lord, bringing forth qualities such as wisdom, understanding, counsel, might, knowledge, and fear of the Lord (Isa 11:2). Similar to how the Spirit once rested upon David, it will also empower the Messiah for his divine role, ensuring harmony "between the will of God and that of the king."[55]

---

51. Gentry, *Postmillennialism*, 19.

52. The word קִנְאַת can be defined as the jealousy of God for his people, especially in battle (cf. Isa 42:13). Brown et al., *Lexicon*, 888.

53. Jamieson et al., *Commentary*, 2:1:601.

54. Kaiser, *Isaiah 1–12*, 157.

55. Kaiser, *Isaiah 1–12*, 157.

According to Gill, the phrase "the earth shall be full of the knowledge of the LORD" symbolizes a time when the gospel message will be widespread and deeply understood. It speaks to the abundance and depth of knowledge about divine matters, particularly about Christ's teachings, grace, righteousness, and salvation.[56] This understanding will be so profound that it will bring peace and security to the people of God. It implies a universal recognition of God's sovereignty and authority, leading to a world characterized by righteousness and the absence of violence.

In verse 10, the "root of Jesse," referring to the Messiah, is identified as a "signal" (נֵס, *nes*) or banner for all nations.[57] The reference, notes Alexander, points to Christ's revelation to the gentiles through the proclamation of the gospel. When it says, "of him shall the nations inquire," it does not merely suggest a superficial curiosity or seeking favor, nor does it imply simply paying religious respects. Rather, it signifies consulting him as a source of all religious truth.[58] The phrase "his resting place" denotes his abode or dwelling, i.e., the church (Eph 2:22; 1 Cor 3:16; Col 1:27).

Verses 11–12 prophesy a future time when the gospel will unite all of God's chosen people globally, including the eventual conversion of the Jews (Rom 11:12–25).[59] Isaiah 65:17–25 expands on this vision, depicting a glorious state of the church. This period, often described as "new heavens and a new earth" (65:17), signifies heightened spiritual blessings leading to societal renewal.[60] John Jefferson Davis argues that this renewal reflects a profound moral transformation of society, similar to Paul's concept of salvation as a "new creation" (2 Cor 5:17). He emphasizes that these blessings in Isa 65:17–25 represent the messianic age when Christ reigns from

---

56. Gill, *Books of the Prophets*, 67.

57. In ancient times, banners served as a means of summoning armies or indicating muster points or camp locations. They often displayed the insignia of a tribe or division. For example, in the Egyptian army, divisions were named after various gods, and banners would represent these gods to identify the division. Walton et al., *IVP Bible Background Commentary*, 600–601; Brown et al., *Lexicon*, 651.

58. Alexander, *Isaiah*, 168–69.

59. Gentry, *Postmillennialism*, 19.

60. This statement refers to the profound moral transformation of society rather than focusing on an eternal state. Isaiah describes a period where children are still being born (v. 20), where individuals continue to build houses and plant vineyards (v. 21), and engage in their earthly tasks (v. 22). Davis, *Christ's Victorious Kingdom*, 37–38.

heaven, rather than exclusively the eternal state or the time after his second coming.[61]

Isaiah 65

> For behold, I create new heavens and a new earth, and the former things shall not be remembered or come into mind.... No more shall there be in it an infant who lives but a few days, or an old man who does not fill out his days, for the young man shall die a hundred years old, and the sinner a hundred years old shall be accursed.... They shall not labor in vain or bear children for calamity, for they shall be the offspring of the blessed of the LORD, and their descendants with them. (Isa 65:17, 20, 23)

Gentry highlights the distinctive perspective of postmillennial eschatology, which emphasizes the transformative impact of Christ's redemptive work within history. He contrasts this with premillennial and amillennial views, which either postpone the full effects of redemption to the end of history or remove them to realms outside of historical existence.[62] Gentry suggests that Isaiah's vision of the "gospel economy's historical impact," as depicted in Isa 65:17–25, provides a framework for understanding the progressive transformation of the world towards the new heavens and new earth. He also connects this vision with Paul's statement in 2 Cor 5:17 about being a new creation in Christ, echoing Davis's view.[63]

Mathison adds to the discussion by noting different interpretations of Isa 65:17–25 among Reformed commentators, with amillennialists viewing it as a prophecy of the eternal state and postmillennialists interpreting it as describing blessings for the present millennial age.[64] Mathison suggests that elements of both interpretations may be present in the prophecy without clear distinction. The following excerpt from Mathison will provide further explanation:

> 1. *New Heavens and a New Earth.* This kind of language can be used as a description of ongoing change in the existing state of affairs (cf. 2 Cor. 5:17; Gal. 6:15), but it is also used to describe

---

61. Davis, *Christ's Victorious Kingdom*, 38.
62. Gentry, *He Shall Have Dominion*, 368.
63. Gentry, *He Shall Have Dominion*, 368.
64. Mathison, *Postmillennialism*, 87.

the state of affairs after the final judgment (2 Peter 3:13). In other words, there is an element of the new creation that is "already" fulfilled in the New Testament age as well as an element that is "not yet" fulfilled. During this period, there is an ongoing work of "re-creation" or sanctification.

2. *Preconsummation Conditions.* This prophecy describes conditions that can hardly apply to the eternal state. For example, birth, death, aging, time, sin, and accursedness are all mentioned in verse 20. Construction and agriculture are mentioned in verses 21 and 22. But although these are all elements of the preconsummation stage of the new creation, they are described as taking place in a radically restored creation.

3. *Edenic Conditions.* Verse 23 describes a state in which the original curse on labor and childbirth has been reversed and God's original purposes for creation are being fulfilled. God originally created man to have dominion over the earth and all the creatures of the earth (Gen. 1:26–28) and to have eternal union and communion with Him in Paradise (Gen. 2:15–17). This prophecy describes the accomplishment of that purpose.[65]

In short, Mathison discusses the concept of the new heavens and new earth by highlighting the dual meaning of ongoing change and the ultimate state after judgment. He notes pre-consummation conditions indicating a restoration within the existing creation, suggesting a return to Edenic conditions where God's original purposes are fulfilled. Furthermore, he argues for the continuity between the present world and the fulfillment of God's promises, implying that these will be realized here unless "clear evidence" can be produced to prove otherwise.[66]

Jeremiah 31

Behold, the days are coming, declares the Lord, when I will make a new covenant with the house of Israel and the house of Judah, not like the covenant that I made with their fathers on the day when I took them by the hand to bring them out of the land of Egypt, my covenant that they broke, though I was their husband, declares the Lord. For this is the covenant that I will make with the house of Israel after those days, declares the Lord: I will put

---

65. Mathison, *Postmillennialism*, 87.
66. Mathison, *Postmillennialism*, 88.

my law within them, and I will write it on their hearts. And I will be their God, and they shall be my people. And no longer shall each one teach his neighbor and each his brother, saying, "Know the LORD," for they shall all know me, from the least of them to the greatest, declares the LORD. For I will forgive their iniquity, and I will remember their sin no more. (Jer 31:31–34)

Jeremiah began his ministry around 627 BC, in the thirteenth year of Josiah's reign, and concluded around 587 BC, during the eleventh year of Zedekiah's rule and the second deportation (Jer 1:1–3; cf. 2 Kgs 22:1; 2 Chr 36:11–21). He ministered during a violent period in Israel's history, particularly during the decline of the Southern Kingdom of Judah before its fall to Babylon.[67] In chapter 31, God promises to establish a new covenant with his people, one where he takes the initiative to bring about the needed internal transformation of the heart. This new covenant addresses the shortcomings of the old covenant, which lacked the power to instigate the internal changes essential for obedience.[68]

In verses 31–34, Jeremiah prophesies a future transformation where God himself will instigate a radical change in his people's inner nature. This change will eradicate their previous inability to adhere to his laws, replacing it with both the desire and capability to obey.[69] This will lead to forgiveness of their sins and iniquities, with God promising not to remember their transgressions anymore. H. D. Potter draws attention to the repetition of the words "iniquity" (עָוֹן, avon) and "sin" (חַטָּאת, hatta't) in the same sequence in Jer 5:25, highlighting the significance of these concepts in hindering God's blessings from his people.[70]

Potter observes the importance of the role of the "heart" (לֵב, leb) in this context as the Hebrew word לֵב is mentioned several times in the preceding verses (5:20–25). The people are described as lacking understanding, despite God's generosity, and their consciousness (לֵבָב, lebab) remains unaffected.[71] The root cause of their rebellion is identified as their stubborn and rebellious "heart" (לֵב). The concept of the new covenant, which is promised to be written on the heart, is presented as a solution to this inherent human nature problem, suggesting a transformation of the heart,

---

67. Walton et al., *IVP Bible Background Commentary*, 642.
68. Mathison, *Postmillennialism*, 88–89.
69. Harrison, *Jeremiah and Lamentations*, 137; Nicholson, *Jeremiah 26–52*, 71.
70. Potter, "New Covenant," 351.
71. Potter, "New Covenant," 351.

leading to a deeper understanding of God and a departure from stubbornness and rebellion.[72]

Mathison notes that the relevance of the new covenant to eschatology lies in its inauguration by Christ during his first coming and its fulfillment through the church in the current age (Luke 22:20; 2 Cor 3:4–6; Heb 7:22; 8:6–13; 9:15; 10:14–18, 29; 12:22–24). This covenant spans the period between the two advents and is not contingent upon "the Millennium or the eternal state."[73] Gentry observes that Jeremiah anticipates a future where the ark of the covenant is forgotten, and all nations gather before the Lord's throne, even historically adversarial ones such as Moab, Ammon, and Elam (Jer 3:16–17; 48:7; 49:6, 39; cf. Isa 19:23–25).[74]

Ezekiel 47

> Then he brought me back to the door of the temple, and behold, water was issuing from below the threshold of the temple toward the east (for the temple faced east). The water was flowing down from below the south end of the threshold of the temple, south of the altar. Then he brought me out by way of the north gate and led me around on the outside to the outer gate that faces toward the east; and behold, the water was trickling out on the south side. Going on eastward with a measuring line in his hand, the man measured a thousand cubits, and then led me through the water, and it was ankle-deep. Again he measured a thousand, and led me through the water, and it was knee-deep. Again he measured a thousand, and led me through the water, and it was waist-deep. Again he measured a thousand, and it was a river that I could not pass through, for the water had risen. It was deep enough to swim in, a river that could not be passed through. And he said to me, "Son of man, have you seen this?" Then he led me back to the bank of the river. As I went back, I saw on the bank of the river very many trees on the one side and on the other. And he said to me, "This water flows toward the eastern region and goes down into the Arabah, and enters the sea; when the water flows into the sea, the water will become fresh. And wherever the river goes, every living creature that swarms will live, and there will be very many fish. For this water goes there, that the waters of the sea may

---

72. Potter, "New Covenant," 351.
73. Mathison, *Postmillennialism*, 90.
74. Gentry, *Postmillennialism*, 19.

become fresh; so everything will live where the river goes." (Ezek 47:1–9)

The symbolism of a river flowing from beneath the threshold of the temple, nourishing the desolate regions of the Dead Sea valley, holds major theological significance. It reflects the Old Testament's depiction of divine blessings intertwined with concepts of fertility and water (Pss 46:4; 65:9; Isa 33:20–24.).[75] The once stagnant waters of the Dead Sea are revitalized, teeming with life, illustrating the transformative power of God's provision. At the heart of this imagery lies the temple, symbolizing life, healing, and abundance.

In the Gospel of John, Jesus identifies himself as the fulfillment of this prophecy, drawing parallels between himself and the temple (John 2:19–21).[76] He declares himself as the source of living water, symbolizing spiritual sustenance and renewal (7:38), exemplified by his pierced side from which blood and water flowed (19:34).[77] Jesus' promise of living water in John 4:14 emphasizes his role as the ultimate source of spiritual nourishment.

The river's gradual growth, starting as a trickle and swelling into a mighty stream, symbolizes the progression of God's redemptive plan. This progression began with the outpouring of the Holy Spirit at Pentecost, signifying the ongoing work of God's Spirit in the world (cf. Acts 2:33).[78] In essence, the imagery of the river in Ezekiel and its connection to Christ's teachings highlights the gradual development of God's redemptive kingdom.

Daniel 2

> You saw, O king, and behold, a great image. This image, mighty and of exceeding brightness, stood before you, and its appearance was frightening. The head of this image was of fine gold, its chest and arms of silver, its middle and thighs of bronze, its legs of iron, its feet partly of iron and partly of clay. As you looked, a stone was cut out by no human hand, and it struck the image on its feet of iron and clay, and broke them in pieces. Then the iron, the clay, the bronze, the silver, and the gold, all together were broken in

---

75. Taylor, *Ezekiel*, 278.
76. Gentry, *He Shall Have Dominion*, 263–64.
77. Henry, *Commentary*, 4:1008.
78. Mathison, *Postmillennialism*, 92.

pieces, and became like the chaff of the summer threshing floors; and the wind carried them away, so that not a trace of them could be found. But the stone that struck the image became a great mountain and filled the whole earth.... And in the days of those kings the God of heaven will set up a kingdom that shall never be destroyed, nor shall the kingdom be left to another people. It shall break in pieces all these kingdoms and bring them to an end, and it shall stand forever. (Dan 2:31–35, 44)

In this prophetic vision, King Nebuchadnezzar witnesses a grand image comprised of distinct materials, emblematic of successive empires: Babylon, Medo-Persia, Greece, and Rome. Each empire is represented by varying elements—gold, silver, bronze, and iron respectively—symbolizing their temporal power and influence.[79] Notably, the feet of the image, composed of iron mixed with clay, depict a combination of strength and weakness. The imagery extends further as the image's destruction unfolds through the intervention of a stone, uncut by human hands. This pivotal moment signifies the ultimate demise of earthly kingdoms, supplanted by the establishment of God's eternal kingdom. The stone, representative of God's kingdom, is inaugurated through the first advent of Christ (cf. Matt 4:17; 12:27–29).[80]

In verse 44, the establishment of God's kingdom is prophesied to coincide with the period of the fourth kingdom, identified as the Roman Empire, as stated above. Sandlin states, "The everlasting kingdom God was to establish in the earth begins when the stone collides with the image's feet. . . . During the Roman Empire God launched his final, impregnable kingdom in the earth."[81] As this kingdom unfolds, it gradually expands until it encompasses the entirety of the globe, symbolizing the pervasive influence of God's sovereignty through the dissemination of the gospel. This process

---

79. Many commentators agree on the symbolic representation of Babylon, Medo-Persia, Greece, and Rome in the text, but interpretations vary. Some suggest the four segments represented Neo-Babylonian kings rather than kingdoms. There is also debate over whether the author of Daniel may have mistakenly substituted Assyria for Babylon. As noted by Storms, non-conservative scholars, often labeled as "liberal critics," date the book to the second century BC and interpret the kingdoms as Babylon, Media, Persia, and Greece, rejecting its prophetic nature. Storms, *Kingdom Come*, 95; Newsom, *Daniel*, 63; Porteous, *Daniel*, 46–47; Swim, "Daniel," 634; Meadowcroft, "Metaphor, Narrative, Interpretation," 265; Davies, "Daniel Chapter Two," 397.

80. Poole, *Commentary*, 2:817; Rogers, *In the Days of These Kings*, 49–51; Rogers, *Prophecy of Daniel*, 21–23.

81. Sandlin, *Postmillennial Primer*, 39.

of expansion is perceived as both gradual and inevitable, ultimately leading to a future era wherein the majority of humanity embraces Christianity and submits to the lordship of Christ.[82]

Mathison outlines the key features of the messianic kingdom as described in the book of Daniel. First, he argues that the kingdom of Christ began during the Roman Empire, rejecting the idea of its establishment in a distant future. Second, he highlights its indestructibility, echoing Jesus' promise that the "gates of hell shall not prevail against it" (Matt 16:18). Third, the kingdom is prophesied to overcome all opposition and eventually encompass the whole world, symbolizing the defeat of all the enemies of God. Finally, he notes its growth is depicted as gradual yet unstoppable, starting small but expanding until it covers the entire earth.[83]

Daniel 7

> I saw in the night visions, and behold, with the clouds of heaven there came one like a son of man, and he came to the Ancient of Days and was presented before him. And to him was given dominion and glory and a kingdom, that all peoples, nations, and languages should serve him; his dominion is an everlasting dominion, which shall not pass away, and his kingdom one that shall not be destroyed. (Dan 7:13–14)

In Daniel's vision, he witnesses a series of symbolic representations, notably various beasts symbolizing different kingdoms, which parallels Nebuchadnezzar's earlier vision in Dan 2.[84] The narrative progresses from these earthly kingdoms to a divine scene where God, referred to as the Ancient of Days, presides on a judgment throne. Amidst this celestial scene, Daniel beholds a figure described as "one like a son of man" approaching with the clouds of heaven, symbolizing Jesus Christ. This term, "son of man," was a significant messianic title used by Jesus to describe himself (Matt 16:13–16; 24:30; 26:64).

Premillennialist scholars tend to interpret this text as referring to the second coming of Christ.[85] However, a close analysis of the context suggests

---

82. Henry, *Commentary*, 4:1032.
83. Mathison, *Postmillennialism*, 94.
84. Elwell, *Commentary*, 596. See also Allis, *Prophecy and the Church*, 125.
85. Walvoord, *Millennial Kingdom*, 267.

otherwise. Mathison points out that the vision unfolds in a heavenly setting, not an earthly one.[86] The imagery portrays the Son of Man *ascending* to the presence of the Ancient of Days in the clouds of heaven (cf. Acts 1:9), resembling Christ's ascension more than his anticipated return.[87]

He is given dominion, glory, and a kingdom by the Father, signifying the authority and reign of Christ over all creation. This is a depiction of Jesus' current reign in heaven, which began with his ascension and will continue until all enemies are subdued under his feet (1 Cor 15:25). The dominion given to the Son of Man is described as everlasting and universal, encompassing all peoples, nations, and languages, indicating that his kingdom is not limited to a particular ethnicity or geographical region. The parallel in Dan 2:35, where the stone grows into a mountain and fills the entire earth, illustrates the gradual expansion and universality of his kingdom.

Zechariah 9

> Rejoice greatly, O daughter of Zion! Shout aloud, O daughter of Jerusalem! Behold, your king is coming to you; righteous and having salvation is he, humble and mounted on a donkey, on a colt, the foal of a donkey. I will cut off the chariot from Ephraim and the war horse from Jerusalem; and the battle bow shall be cut off, and he shall speak peace to the nations; his rule shall be from sea to sea, and from the River to the ends of the earth. (Zech 9:9–10)

The immediate fulfillment of this prophecy is seen in the triumphal entry of Jesus into Jerusalem (Matt 21:1–11), where he entered as a humble king riding on a donkey. The imagery of cutting off chariots, war horses, and battle bows symbolizes the cessation of warfare and the establishment of peace under the reign of the Messiah.[88] This speaks to the transformative power of Christ's kingdom, which extends not just to Israel but to all nations ("he shall speak peace to the nations").[89]

---

86. Mathison, *Postmillennialism*, 95. See also Dumbrell, *Search for Order*, 142.

87. Rogers, *Prophecy of Daniel*, 24; Sandlin, *Postmillennial Primer*, 39–40.

88. Hill, *Haggai, Zechariah and Malachi*, 210. See also Petersen, *Zechariah 9–14 and Malachi*, 59.

89. Mathison observes that this prophecy echoes the certainty expressed in Ps 72, affirming that the reign of Christ will encompass the entirety of the earth. Mathison, *Postmillennialism*, 99.

The phrase "his rule shall be from sea to sea, and from the River to the ends of the earth" indicates the universal extent of Christ's reign. This is indicative of the gradual expansion of the gospel and the influence of Christ's kingdom throughout history, leading to a time of widespread peace and righteousness on earth before his return. As Thomas Verner Moore states, "That the tendencies of Christ's kingdom are to universal peace and universal piety, we need not pause to argue, and that these tendencies shall yet be fully embodied, we believe as well from the voice of history as from the word of prophecy. We have only to patiently labor, and patiently wait, and the white banner of the lowly king shall in due time be unfurled from every mountain-top."[90] Thus, the prophecy regarding the triumphal entry of Jesus into Jerusalem serves as a poignant illustration of the transformative power and universal reach of his kingdom.

SUMMARY

This chapter has examined the portrayal of the Messiah's reign over an expansive earthly kingdom as depicted in the Psalms and the Prophets within the Old Testament. Through an exegetical analysis of key passages, the chapter has highlighted the optimism and postmillennial hope embedded in these texts. Psalms 2, 22, and 110 clearly depict the Messiah's authority, the ultimate triumph over opposition, and the global recognition of God's sovereignty.

Likewise, the prophets, including Isaiah, Jeremiah, Ezekiel, Daniel, and Zechariah, present prophetic visions of a future where peace, justice, and righteousness prevail under the Messiah's reign. While not exhaustive, this chapter has shown how these visions emphasize the gradual expansion of Christ's kingdom, the transformative power of the gospel, and the eventual fulfillment of God's redemptive plan for all nations. The following chapter will further support this notion by exploring corresponding themes within the New Testament.

---

90. Moore, *Commentary on Zechariah*, 150–51.

Chapter Four

New Testament Foundations

NEW TESTAMENT

The New Testament offers numerous passages emphasizing the postmillennial expectation of the gospel's ultimate triumph and the establishment of Christ's kingdom on the earth. This chapter directs its attention to such passages within the Gospel of Matthew, the book of Acts, and the Epistles. While recognizing that the postmillennial hope is also portrayed in the Gospels of Mark, Luke and John, this study will primarily concentrate on the gradual expansion of the kingdom as outlined in the Gospel of Matthew. The Olivet Discourse, given its significance to the study, will be discussed separately in chapter 5. The book of Revelation will be discussed in chapters 6 and 7.

The Gospel of Matthew

The Lord's Prayer

> Our Father in heaven, hallowed be your name. Your kingdom come, your will be done, on earth as it is in heaven. Give us this day our daily bread, and forgive us our debts, as we also have forgiven our debtors. And lead us not into temptation, but deliver us from evil. (Matt 6:9–13)

In teaching his disciples to pray, Jesus includes the petition, "Your kingdom come, your will be done, on earth as it is in heaven." This prayer reflects a desire for the complete realization of God's sovereignty on earth, where his divine purpose is perfectly accomplished. This sentiment is echoed in the ministry of John the Baptist, who initiated his message with an urgent call to repentance, proclaiming, "Repent, for the kingdom of heaven is at hand" (Matt 3:2). Similarly, Jesus inaugurated his earthly ministry with the same proclamation, urging repentance for the imminent arrival of the kingdom of heaven (4:17).[1]

R. C. Sproul emphasizes that the "kingdom of God" is a central motif that unifies the narratives of both the Old and New Testaments. He notes that at the core of this theme lies the anticipation of God's messianic kingdom, governed by his appointed Messiah, who not only serves as the redeemer of his people but also assumes the role as their king.[2] In Matt 6:10, Jesus instructs his disciples to pray for the fulfillment of God's will on earth, mirroring its realization in heaven.

Sproul observes that while the concept of God's will has various meanings throughout Scripture, it is most commonly used in two primary senses: the sovereign, efficacious will of God and the prescriptive will of God.[3] Sproul argues that when Jesus directs his disciples to pray for the fulfillment of God's will, he refers to the prescriptive aspect, which entails obedience to divine commands, echoing the continuous obedience observed by the angels in heaven. Thus, each recitation of the Lord's Prayer invokes a plea for divine assistance in aligning one's actions with God's will on earth, as it is faithfully obeyed in heaven. This highlights the imperative for believers not to passively await the eschatological fulfillment of God's kingdom but to actively participate in its manifestation by adhering to his will.[4]

In his commentary, Poole articulates a similar sentiment, advocating for the universal reign of the Lord over all nations and the voluntary submission of humanity to his divine laws, as well as the proclamation and advancement of the gospel of the kingdom.[5] He envisions a state where God's will is executed on earth with the same fervor and willingness exhibited by

---

1. In the Gospel of Matthew, the terms "kingdom of heaven" and "kingdom of God" are used interchangeably, as seen in 19:23–24 and through Matthew's consistent use of "kingdom of heaven" where the other gospels use "kingdom of God" (e.g., Matt 4:17 and Mark 1:15; Matt 13:31–33 and Mark 4:30–32). McIver, "Parable of the Weeds," 644.

2. Sproul, *Matthew*, 128.

3. Sproul, *Matthew*, 130–31. For more information on the nuances of the will of God, see E. F. Harrison, "Will," in Elwell, *Evangelical Dictionary of Theology*, 1275; Erickson, *Christian Theology*, 334.

4. Sproul, *Matthew*, 131.

5. Poole, *Commentary*, 3:27.

the angels and saints in heaven.[6] In essence, the Lord's Prayer expresses the postmillennial hope for the eventual establishment of Christ's kingdom on earth in its entirety.

Parable of the Mustard Seed

> He put another parable before them, saying, "The kingdom of heaven is like a grain of mustard seed that a man took and sowed in his field. It is the smallest of all seeds, but when it has grown it is larger than all the garden plants and becomes a tree, so that the birds of the air come and make nests in its branches." (Matt 13:31–32)

In this passage, Jesus employs the imagery of the mustard seed, a tiny seed that grows into a large tree, to illustrate the expansive nature of the kingdom of heaven. This imagery of exponential growth echoes prophetic motifs found in the Old Testament, such as the stone from heaven that grew into a great mountain (Dan 2:31–35, 44) and the water flowing from the temple that widened and deepened into a mighty river (Ezek 47:1–9).[7] Through this parable, Jesus conveys three characteristics about the kingdom of God: its humble beginnings, gradual expansion, and eventual immensity.[8]

However, this growth does not imply universal acceptance or the absence of opposition. Indeed, as depicted in the parables of the weeds (Matt 13:24–30, 36–43) and the net (13:47–50), the kingdom encompasses both genuine believers and unbelievers (see chapter 9 of the present book for a response to objections pertaining to the postmillennial hope conveyed in these parables). At the second coming of Christ, there will be a decisive separation between the two, with unbelievers facing judgment and expulsion from the kingdom into the lake of fire (Matt 25:31–46; cf. Rev 20:7–15).

Thus, the parable of the mustard seed provided encouragement to Jesus' disciples. It not only clarified the nature of the kingdom but also bolstered their faith amidst adversity.[9] The parable highlights the observable, gradual growth of the kingdom in the world. It emphasizes the optimism

---

6. Poole, *Commentary*, 3:28.
7. Davis, *Christ's Victorious Kingdom*, 49.
8. Sandlin, *Postmillennial Primer*, 45.
9. Davis, *Christ's Victorious Kingdom*, 50.

and hope that characterizes postmillennial eschatology, as well as the belief in the eventual triumph of God's purposes in history.

Parable of the Leaven

> He told them another parable. "The kingdom of heaven is like leaven that a woman took and hid in three measures of flour, till it was all leavened." (Matt 13:33)

Similarly, in the parable of the leaven, Jesus likens the kingdom of heaven to leaven that permeates the entire batch of dough. This imagery suggests the pervasive influence of the gospel, gradually transforming society from within. J. Dwight Pentecost remarks, "Jesus was teaching that the kingdom would not be established by outward means, since no external force could cause the dough to rise. Rather, this new form of the kingdom would operate according to an internal force that would be continuous and progressive until the whole mixture had been leavened."[10] True enough, but this parable also suggests that the kingdom's growth should manifest visibly, like a tree that is known by its fruit (cf. Matt 7:15–20).

The parable of the leaven, like the one about the mustard seed which precedes it, illustrates how something small and seemingly trivial can eventually lead to something significant.[11] Both parables describe the kingdom of God as starting off modestly but eventually having an impact that far exceeds its humble beginnings. The key message of the parable is the extraordinary effect that comes from such modest origins, emphasizing that gradual growth is an essential element of the story.[12]

The Great Commission

> And Jesus came and said to them, "All authority in heaven and on earth has been given to me. Go therefore and make disciples of all nations, baptizing them in the name of the Father and of the Son and of the Holy Spirit, teaching them to observe all that I have commanded you. And behold, I am with you always, to the end of the age." (Matt 28:18–20)

---

10. Pentecost, *Thy Kingdom Come*, 223; Gentry, *He Shall Have Dominion*, 250–51.
11. Mathison, *From Age to Age*, 361–62.
12. Hagner, *Matthew 1–13*, 389–90.

The Great Commission plays a vital role in Christian belief and action. It represents Jesus' last instructions to his followers, detailing the church's purpose until his eventual return. This mandate not only directs the evangelical efforts of Christians but also supports the postmillennial perspective. It emphasizes Christ's authority, the global scope of discipleship, the ethical transformation of societies, and the promise of Christ's continual presence. Therefore, this section argues that these elements uphold the postmillennial belief, foreseeing a future where the gospel triumphs globally before the second advent.

Matthew 28:18 states, "All authority in heaven and on earth has been given to me." This statement indicates Christ's sovereign rule over all creation, implying that his directives carry ultimate power and legitimacy. The Greek word for "authority" here is ἐξουσία (*exousia*), which refers to the right to control or command, the power to act, and the authority to govern.[13] In essence, this verse is emphasizing Christ's ultimate authority over all realms, including the earthly realm which will see the expansion of his kingdom.

Gentry points to the significance of the term "given" in verse 18. He observes that the Greek verb tense indicates the grant of authority occurred at some point in the past.[14] Gentry contends that this best aligns with the pivotal event of the resurrection (cf. Rom 1:4; Phil 2:8–9). The resurrection, followed closely by the ascension, definitively affirmed Christ's sovereignty and his rightful enthronement.

In verse 19, the command to "make disciples of all nations" indicates a mission that goes beyond ethnic, cultural, and geographical boundaries.[15] H. Wayne House and Thomas D. Ice contend that this entails solely

---

13. Alexander Balmain Bruce notes that the Greek term, ἐξουσία, in this verse encompasses every form of authority. It signifies the command over all resources necessary for the "advancement of the kingdom of God." Bruce, "Synoptic Gospels," in Nicoll, *Expositor's Greek Testament*, 1:339. Cf. Danker et al., *Lexicon*, 352–53.

14. Gentry notes that the Greek word for "given" is ἐδόθη (*edothe*), which is in the aorist passive indicative form of δίδωμι (*didomi*). He further notes that the term "aorist" is derived from two Greek words: α, "no" and ὁρίζω, "horizon," indicating that it means "unlimited." Usually, the aorist tense does not specify a particular time. However, in the indicative mood, it implies a past action perceived as occurring at a single point in time. Likewise, Bruce states, "The reference may be to the resurrection, and the meaning that the event *ipso facto* placed Jesus in a position of power." Gentry, *Greatness of the Great Commission*, 32; Alexander Balmain Bruce, "Synoptic Gospels," in Nicoll, *Expositor's Greek Testament*, 1:339.

15. Gentry observes that the directive to go to the nations contrasts with Christ's

bearing witness to the world, refraining from actual engagement beyond proclaiming the gospel.[16] However, Christ's directive extends further, requiring the discipling of all nations by "teaching them to observe all that I have commanded you," rather than merely witnessing to them (Matt 28:20). Loraine Boettner states,

> We believe that the Great Commission includes not merely the formal and external announcement of the Gospel preached as a "witness" to the nations, as the Premillennialists and Amillennialists hold, but the true and effectual evangelization of all the nations so that the hearts and lives of the people are transformed by it. . . . The disciples were commanded not merely to preach, but *to make disciples of all the nations*. It was no doubtful experiment to which they were called, but to assure triumph.[17]

The Greek term for "teaching" (διδάσκοντες, *didaskontes*) conveys the notion of instructing or imparting knowledge in a formal or informal setting.[18] This mandate highlights the ethical dimension of discipleship, wherein converts are not only baptized but also instructed to embody Christ's teachings in their lives.

The passage's concluding words, "And behold, I am with you always, to the end of the age," offer assurance and encouragement for the church's mission. This promise of continuous presence ensures that the efforts to disciple the nations are supported and guided by divine assistance. Empowered by Christ's authority and assured of his support, the church's mission is destined for success (see chapter 9 for a response to objections regarding the postmillennial understanding of the Great Commission).[19]

---

earlier command to "Go nowhere among the Gentiles" (Matt 10:5–6). While the gospel was initially intended for the Jews, it was always part of God's plan to incorporate gentiles into the kingdom (cf. Isa 49:6; 60:3; Rom 1:16; Gal 3:28). Gentry, *Greatness of the Great Commission*, 49.

16. House and Ice, *Dominion Theology*, 165.
17. Boettner, *Millennium*, 15 (emphasis original).
18. Danker et al., *Lexicon*, 240–41.
19. Mathison, *Postmillennialism*, 116.

The Acts of the Apostles

Acts 2:30–36

> Being therefore a prophet, and knowing that God had sworn with an oath to him that he would set one of his descendants on his throne, he foresaw and spoke about the resurrection of the Christ, that he was not abandoned to Hades, nor did his flesh see corruption. This Jesus God raised up, and of that we all are witnesses. Being therefore exalted at the right hand of God, and having received from the Father the promise of the Holy Spirit, he has poured out this that you yourselves are seeing and hearing. For David did not ascend into the heavens, but he himself says, "The Lord said to my Lord, 'Sit at my right hand, until I make your enemies your footstool.'" Let all the house of Israel therefore know for certain that God has made him both Lord and Christ, this Jesus whom you crucified. (Acts 2:30–36)

In Peter's sermon on the day of Pentecost, following the outpouring of the Holy Spirit upon the disciples, an important emphasis is placed on the realization of Old Testament prophecy through the person of Jesus Christ. Peter connects David's messianic prophecy from Ps 110:1 with the events surrounding Jesus' resurrection and ascension, thereby presenting Christ as the anticipated Messiah seated at the right hand of God.[20] Through the identification of Jesus as the fulfillment of the Davidic lineage and the legitimate heir to David's throne, Peter posits the commencement of the messianic kingdom as a present reality. This assertion stands in contrast to the futurist perspective which argues that the forthcoming establishment of the messianic kingdom is contingent upon the future return of Christ. Thus, Acts 2:30–36 appears to contradict the futurist interpretation, affirming that Jesus currently reigns on the throne of David and will continue to do so until all his adversaries are subjected beneath his feet.

---

20. Peter's proclamation confronts the Jewish dilemma regarding Jesus' lordship over David. By referencing Ps 110:1, which portrays David acknowledging another as his Lord, Peter highlights the paradox of Jesus being both the descendant and Lord of David. The pre-Christian, rabbinic messianic interpretations of Ps 110, combined with the event of Jesus' resurrection, provided early Christians with scriptural validation for claiming Jesus as the Messiah. Psalm 110's exalted language and messianic undertones, recognized by these first-century rabbis, aligned with prevailing expectations of a messianic figure, strengthening the early Christian argument for Jesus' messianic identity. Callan, "Psalm 110:1," 625–26; Hay, *Glory at the Right Hand*, 27–30, 159. See also Davies, *Paul and Rabbinic Judaism*, 161–63.

Sandlin contends that Peter's sermon clarifies that David's references in Ps 110 to the conquering "Son of Jehovah" and in Ps 16 to the resurrection were predictions of Christ's present reign.[21] If Peter had meant that the reign and defeat of God's enemies described in Ps 110 were to occur only at Christ's second coming, Sandlin argues it would not make sense for him to present this psalm as being fulfilled by Christ's death, resurrection, ascension, and enthronement. Instead, Peter's message suggests that the reign of Christ, as foretold in Ps 110, is happening in the current age.[22]

Acts 13:46–47

> And Paul and Barnabas spoke out boldly, saying, "It was necessary that the word of God be spoken first to you. Since you thrust it aside and judge yourselves unworthy of eternal life, behold, we are turning to the Gentiles. For so the Lord has commanded us, saying, 'I have made you a light for the Gentiles, that you may bring salvation to the ends of the earth.'" (Acts 13:46–47)

In Acts 13, Paul and Barnabas embark on a missionary journey to spread the gospel. In the synagogue in Antioch of Pisidia (13:14), Paul boldly proclaims Jesus as the Messiah (13:13–43). However, faced with rejection and opposition from the Jewish audience, Paul declares that they will turn their message to the gentiles, citing the prophecy from Isa 42:6 and 49:6, "I have made you a light for the Gentiles" (Acts 13:44–47). This passage serves as a key moment in the narrative of Acts, symbolizing the expansion of the gospel beyond the confines of Judaism to embrace the gentile world.

Mathison rightly notes that this prophecy is applied to the disciples of Jesus, signifying their covenantal union with him and their mission to extend salvation to all nations.[23] This appointing of the disciples by Jesus reflects the Great Commission in Matt 28:18–20, where Jesus delegates his authority and task of global evangelization to his followers. The church, as the body of Christ, is entrusted with the eschatological task of bearing witness of Jesus to all nations. Through faithful proclamation and discipleship, the church participates in the advancement of God's kingdom on earth.

---

21. Sandlin, *Postmillennial Primer*, 41.

22. Sandlin, *Postmillennial Primer*, 41.

23. Mathison, *Postmillennialism*, 118–19; For deeper insights into the postmillennial perspective depicted in the book of Acts, see Mathison, *From Age to Age*, 452–92.

This echoes the imagery used by Jesus himself, such as the parables of the mustard seed and the leaven, as demonstrated earlier, which depict the gradual but transformative growth of the kingdom. This gradual but inevitable growth reflects the fulfillment of God's covenant promises to Abraham to bless all the families of the earth through his offspring (Gen 12:3).

The Epistles

Romans 11:11–26

> So I ask, did they stumble in order that they might fall? By no means! Rather, through their trespass salvation has come to the Gentiles, so as to make Israel jealous. Now if their trespass means riches for the world, and if their failure means riches for the Gentiles, how much more will their full inclusion mean! (Rom 11:11–12)

In this passage, Paul employs a rhetorical question: "Did they stumble in order that they might fall?" He answers emphatically, "By no means!" Through the preceding chapters, Paul described Israel's collective rejection of the Messiah and failure to embrace their divine calling due to their adherence to a doctrine of works righteousness, resulting in a spiritual blindness.[24] Paul explains that Israel's stumbling is not meant to cause their downfall but rather to pave the way for the salvation of the gentiles. This, in turn, will stir jealousy in Israel and eventually lead to their own redemption.

> Now I am speaking to you Gentiles. Inasmuch then as I am an apostle to the Gentiles, I magnify my ministry in order somehow to make my fellow Jews jealous, and thus save some of them. For if their rejection means the reconciliation of the world, what will their acceptance mean but life from the dead? (Rom 11:13–15)

The Lord had appointed Paul as a minister of the gospel, equipping him for this role, and elevating him to the position of an apostle. Through his ministry, Paul had become invaluable to both Jews and gentiles. Being

---

24. Paul recounts Israel's historical disobedience despite their covenant status (Rom 9:6–29), emphasizing their reliance on the law over faith in Christ (9:30—10:4). This leads to spiritual blindness, hindering recognition of Jesus' role in prophecy fulfillment. He contrasts gentiles' faith-based righteousness with Jews stumbling over Christ (9:30–33; 11:11–12). Murray, *Epistle to the Romans*, xii–xv. See also Mathison, *Postmillennialism*, 121–30; Sproul, *Romans*, 339–45.

a Jew himself, Paul understood that God had not completely rejected all ethnic Jews, as a remnant still remained (11:1). Yet, the rejection of the Jews had resulted in significant benefits for the gentiles, but their acceptance and restoration would bring even greater blessings.[25]

The phrase "life from the dead" signifies a remarkable positive transformation. The conversion of Israel would revitalize aspects of the Christian church that were faltering, strengthening the faith of the gentiles and fostering unity among them, initiating a spiritual renewal and reform.[26] Robert H. Gundry argues, "The coming acceptance of Israel as an ethnic whole will entail 'life from among the dead,' that is, resurrection to eternal life. Since the resurrection will occur at Christ's second coming, so too will Israel's acceptance by God; and the resurrection to eternal life will constitute the gentiles greater 'wealth' of which 11:12 spoke."[27] In other words, it anticipates a future where Israel's acceptance sparks a widespread spiritual revival, akin to a resurrection.

> If the dough offered as firstfruits is holy, so is the whole lump, and if the root is holy, so are the branches. But if some of the branches were broken off, and you, although a wild olive shoot, were grafted in among the others and now share in the nourishing root of the olive tree, do not be arrogant toward the branches. If you are, remember it is not you who support the root, but the root that supports you. Then you will say, "Branches were broken off so that I might be grafted in." That is true. They were broken off because of their unbelief, but you stand fast through faith. So do not become proud, but fear. For if God did not spare the natural branches, neither will he spare you. (Rom 11:16–21)

The Israelites were commanded to offer the first produce of their land to God, both in its unprocessed form as a sheaf of newly harvested grain (Lev 23:10–11) and in its processed form as loaves of dough (Num 15:19–21). This practice symbolized the consecration of the entire harvest season to God. The apostle Paul draws on this imagery of firstfruits to illustrate the sanctity and separation of the Israelites as a whole nation, suggesting that just as the firstfruits were set apart, so too was Israel throughout history.[28]

---

25. Gill, *Exposition of the New Testament*, 2:484.
26. Poole, *Commentary*, 3:518.
27. Gundry, *Commentary*, 611.
28. Jamieson et al., *Commentary*, 3:2:259.

Paul then employs the imagery of an olive tree to represent the covenant community of God.[29] He explains that most of ethnic Israel, having rejected the Messiah, are like branches broken off from the tree. In contrast, believing gentiles are compared to "wild" olive branches that have been grafted into the healthy olive tree. Paul admonishes the gentiles not to boast about their inclusion, emphasizing that their place in the olive tree is entirely due to God's grace.[30]

In essence, Paul argues that gentile believers, or Christians, are grafted into the faith, becoming part of true Israel, to replace the ethnic Jews who rejected the Messiah. However, he asserts that the Jews are not permanently excluded from God's redemptive plan. The calling of the gentiles serves as a means to provoke jealousy among the Jews, ultimately leading to their conversion (Rom 11:11–12, 23–25). Paul consistently refers to believing gentiles as being the true Jews by faith (Rom 2:28–29; 9:6–9, 22–30; Gal 6:15–16). Thus, Christians are true Israelites, heirs of God's promises through faith in Christ, regardless of ethnicity (cf. Gal 3:23–29).

> Note then the kindness and the severity of God: severity toward those who have fallen, but God's kindness to you, provided you continue in his kindness. Otherwise you too will be cut off. And even they, if they do not continue in their unbelief, will be grafted in, for God has the power to graft them in again. For if you were cut from what is by nature a wild olive tree, and grafted, contrary to nature, into a cultivated olive tree, how much more will these, the natural branches, be grafted back into their own olive tree. (Rom 11:22–24)

Paul continues the analogy of an olive tree to illustrate the relationship between God, Israel, and the gentiles. He argues that the natural branches (ethnic Jews) can be easily grafted back into their own olive tree, highlighting the expectation of their future restoration. Gentry argues that this

---

29. Craig S. Keener notes that in Jewish tradition, Israel is often symbolized as a plant or tree with roots tracing back to the patriarchs. This imagery includes references to an olive tree, such as a synagogue in Rome being named the "olive tree." However, Paul's teachings departed from conventional Jewish beliefs by asserting that uncircumcised gentiles could join the people of God through faith in the Jewish Messiah. This idea draws parallels with the practice of grafting trees, a technique mentioned in both Jewish and Greco-Roman texts. Grafting involves attaching a shoot from one tree onto another, sometimes using shoots from a wild olive tree to revive a domestic olive tree struggling to bear fruit. Keener, *Background Commentary*, 447. Cf. Pliny the Elder, *Natural History*, 17.10.

30. Mathison, *Postmillennialism*, 125; Sproul, *Romans*, 343–44.

analogy demonstrates that God's rejection of Israel is neither total nor final. At present, a remnant of Israel remains according to the election of grace (Rom 11:5), demonstrating that God's covenantal promises are still in effect. Gentry further observes that the current hardening of some in Israel serves a divine purpose, allowing the inclusion of gentiles (11:7–10).[31]

However, this hardening is temporary, as Paul foresees a future where God will bring the Jews back into his favor, placing them in an equal position with the saved gentiles (11:11–26). Dispensationalist John MacArthur supports this view, noting that Israel will eventually repent and embrace the Messiah (Zech 12:10), and God will "gladly graft the (believing) Jewish people back into the olive tree of His covenant blessings."[32] Thus, the presence of a remnant indicates that God's rejection is not total, and the anticipated restoration of Israel shows that his rejection is not final, affirming the continuity and fulfillment of God's redemptive plan.[33]

> Lest you be wise in your own sight, I do not want you to be unaware of this mystery, brothers: a partial hardening has come upon Israel, until the fullness of the Gentiles has come in. And in this way all Israel will be saved, as it is written, "The Deliverer will come from Zion, he will banish ungodliness from Jacob." (Rom 11:25–26)

In verse 25, Paul extends a sincere message to the gentile believers, addressing them as "brothers" to express his deep affection and concern for their spiritual growth.[34] He emphasizes his desire for them to grasp a profound truth, stating, "I do not want you to be unaware." This truth revolves around a "mystery" previously concealed but now revealed regarding the relationship between Israel and the gentiles in God's overarching plan. The "blindness" that has affected Israel refers to their spiritual unbelief and inability to recognize Jesus as the Messiah, a condition decreed by God, a "partial hardening." This blindness serves as a judgment for their rejection

---

31. Gentry, *Postmillennialism*, 35.
32. MacArthur, *Bible Commentary*, 1543.
33. Chilton, *Paradise Restored*, 129.
34. In the early church, the term "brother" (ἀδελφός, *adelphos*) symbolized love and unity among believers (cf. Acts 9:17; 1 Cor 1:10; Heb 13:1). Biblical writers often used family imagery to illustrate how the gospel transforms lives. Jesus' teaching on being "born again" (John 3:3, 5) signifies a spiritual rebirth into God's family. Consequently, believers, recognizing God as their Father, are called to regard one another as family—fathers, mothers, brothers, and sisters (1 Tim 5:1–2). Youngblood, *Dictionary*, 206, 397.

of Christ, as foretold in various Old Testament Scriptures (cf. Deut 29:4; Ps 69:22–23; Isa 6:9–10; 29:10).[35]

Paul clarifies that this blindness is not total, as there remains a remnant of believing Jews. However, the majority of Israel remains in this state until "the fullness of the Gentiles has come in," possibly meaning until the complete number of gentiles chosen by God for salvation has been reached. Ultimately, Paul suggests a future time when both Jews and gentiles will come together in faith, envisioning a time of great spiritual awakening and the fulfillment of God's plan for all nations to worship him.[36]

Verse 26 holds the phrase "all Israel will be saved," which carries interpretations suggesting a spiritual Israel, inclusive of both Jews and gentiles, according to John Calvin and Augustine of Hippo. Conversely, Charles Hodge, Theodore Beza, and John Gill view it as pertaining to the physical descendants of Israel, representing the Jewish people collectively.[37] Regardless, the present author argues that the verse denotes a future salvation, wherein a significant portion of the Jewish population will turn to God, recognizing Jesus as their Messiah.[38]

1 Corinthians 15:20–28

> But in fact Christ has been raised from the dead, the firstfruits of those who have fallen asleep. For as by a man came death, by a man has come also the resurrection of the dead. For as in Adam all die, so also in Christ shall all be made alive. But each in his own order: Christ the firstfruits, then at his coming those who belong

---

35. Gill, *Exposition of the New Testament*, 2:493–94.
36. Gill, *Exposition of the New Testament*, 2:494.
37. John Calvin interpreted the phrase in a spiritual manner, suggesting it refers to the true Israel of God, encompassing all believers in Christ, whether Jews or gentiles. Charles Hodge, recognizing Calvin and Augustine's spiritual interpretation, sees it differently, viewing it as pertaining to the physical nation of Israel. Theodore Beza argued that there will be a time in which the Jews will "effectually embrace" Jesus as the Messiah. John Gill also understands the phrase as signifying the conversion of a multitude of ethnic Jews to Christianity. Calvin, *Commentaries on the Epistle of Paul the Apostle to the Romans*, 437; Hodge, *Commentary on the Epistle to the Romans*, 374; Beza, *New Testament of Our Lord Jesus Christ*, 67; Gill, *Exposition of the New Testament*, 2:494.
38. Mathison contends that "all Israel" mentioned in verse 26 is synonymous with the Israel described as partially hardened in verse 25. Mathison sees Rom 11:11–32 as referring to a future event involving the extensive restoration of the entire people of Israel to the covenant blessings of salvation. Mathison, *Postmillennialism*, 126–29.

to Christ. Then comes the end, when he delivers the kingdom to God the Father after destroying every rule and every authority and power. For he must reign until he has put all his enemies under his feet. The last enemy to be destroyed is death. For "God has put all things in subjection under his feet." But when it says, "all things are put in subjection," it is plain that he is excepted who put all things in subjection under him. When all things are subjected to him, then the Son himself will also be subjected to him who put all things in subjection under him, that God may be all in all. (1 Cor 15:20–28)

In 1 Cor 15:20–28, Paul emphasizes Christ's present reign and his ultimate victory over all enemies. He begins by explaining the sequence of the resurrection, with Christ being the first to rise from the dead, followed by believers.[39] Just as the firstfruits of a harvest were brought to God as an offering, symbolizing the entire harvest to come, Christ's resurrection serves as the firstfruits of the resurrection to eternal life for believers (cf. Exod 23:29; Lev 23:10). While there were instances of resurrection before him, such as the instances of the widow's son by Elijah (1 Kgs 17:17–24), the Shunammite's son by Elisha (2 Kgs 4:32–37), and Lazarus by Christ (John 11:1–44), these resurrections were temporary and not by their own power.[40]

Christ, however, rose from the dead by his own power and ascended to heaven, presenting himself to God as the representative of his people (Rom 6:9). Thus, believers, as members of Christ, will be raised to eternal life, but this transformation will happen in conjunction with and subsequent to Christ's return. The resurrection of believers culminates in the "end" when Christ delivers the kingdom to God the Father *after* abolishing all opposition. The phrase "he must reign until he has put all his enemies under his feet" implies a gradual process rather than an instantaneous event. In short, Christ's victory in establishing his kingdom must happen *prior* to his second coming, during which he defeats death by resurrecting his followers from the grave (see chapter 9 for a response to objections regarding the postmillennial understanding of 1 Cor 15:24–28).[41]

---

39. Poole, *Commentary*, 3:594.

40. Gill, *Exposition of the New Testament*, 2:673.

41. First Corinthians 15 highlights Christ's active rule and his eventual triumph over all powers, aligning with Old Testament prophecies, emphasizing the victory of the future messianic figure who would reign as king and establish God's kingdom on earth (Ps 110:1; Isa 9:6–7; Dan 7:13–14). Mathison, *Postmillennialism*, 130. See also Gentry, *He Shall Have Dominion*, 257–60.

SUMMARY

The New Testament provides compelling evidence for the postmillennial expectation of the gospel's ultimate triumph and the establishment of Christ's kingdom on earth. This chapter has explored key passages from the Gospel of Matthew, the book of Acts, and the Epistles to demonstrate the postmillennial hope. The Lord's Prayer in Matthew expresses a desire for God's kingdom to fully manifest on earth, while the parables of the mustard seed and the leaven illustrate the kingdom's gradual yet expansive growth. The Great Commission highlights the global scope and ethical transformation envisioned for Christ's followers.

Additionally, the book of Acts emphasizes the present reality of the messianic kingdom through Jesus' resurrection and ascension, and Paul's writings in Romans and 1 Cor 15 highlight the inclusion of gentiles and the future restoration of Israel, ultimately pointing to Christ's reign until all enemies are subdued. While not exhaustive, the aim of this chapter is to demonstrate the pervasive postmillennial hope within the New Testament. The following chapter will further support this idea by exploring corresponding themes within the Olivet Discourse.

Chapter Five

The Olivet Discourse

THE OLIVET DISCOURSE

Many evangelicals interpret Matt 24 as a prophecy signaling the beginning of the "last days" and a global tribulation.[1] However, a critical reassessment of this interpretation is imperative. This present author contends that the passage primarily pertains to the destruction of Jerusalem and the Second Temple, rather than presenting a pessimistic outlook on the end of the world. Therefore, this section will focus on constructing a compelling case to substantiate this thesis.

> Jesus left the temple and was going away, when his disciples came to point out to him the buildings of the temple. But he answered them, "You see all these, do you not? Truly, I say to you, there will not be left here one stone upon another that will not be thrown down." (Matt 24:1–2)

The Olivet Discourse is a sermon given by Jesus Christ on the Mount of Olives, as detailed in Matt 24, Mark 13, and Luke 21.[2] The discourse begins with Jesus predicting the destruction of Jerusalem and the Second

---

1. Many books have been written on the subject of the great tribulation and the end times, frequently citing Matt 24 as a key reference. For example, see LaHaye, *Revelation*, 260; Swaggart, *Armageddon*, v.

2. The Gospel of John omits the Olivet Discourse likely because John addresses the same theme—the destruction of Jerusalem—in his other work, the book of Revelation. Therefore, it may be possible that John did not feel the need to include the Olivet Discourse in his Gospel account, as he had already dedicated an entire book to that subject. For more information pertaining to how Revelation relates to the Olivet Discourse, see Gentry, *He Shall Have Dominion*, 165–66. For information pertaining to the date of the Gospel of John, see Robinson, *Redating*, 254–311.

Temple in response to his disciples' admiration of its magnificence (24:1–2). The disciples then inquire about the timing of these events, to which Jesus responds by cautioning them about future false messiahs, wars, famines, and earthquakes (vv. 3–13).³

The Whole World

Verse 14 states, "And this gospel of the kingdom will be proclaimed throughout the whole world as a testimony to all nations, and then the end will come." At first glance, as Sproul notes, this might seem unfulfilled because there are still remote areas where the gospel has not reached.⁴ However, the apostle Paul indicates otherwise in Col 1:5–6, where he says, "The gospel, which has come to you, as indeed in the whole world it is bearing fruit and increasing." Paul's assertion suggests that by the middle of the first century, the gospel had already been disseminated across the entire "world."⁵

The next step is to understand what is meant by the "whole world" in relation to the spread of the gospel. Mathison argues that the prophecy in Matt 24:14 does not require the gospel to be proclaimed to every individual on the planet. Instead, it refers to a specific historical and geographical context, supported by five key points.⁶ First, the Greek word οἰκουμένη (*oikoumene*), translated as "world" in this verse, often specifically refers to the Roman Empire rather than the entire globe. This is evident in other New Testament passages such as Luke 2:1, where it refers to a decree from Caesar Augustus that "all the world [οἰκουμένη] should be registered," clearly indicating the Roman Empire.⁷

---

3. Josephus documents the rise of various self-proclaimed messianic figures in the period leading up to the Jewish War (*Jewish War*, 2.13). Moreover, historical records from Josephus and Tacitus attest to the occurrence of significant famines and earthquakes during the first century, aligning with Jesus' prophetic predictions (Josephus, *Antiquities*, 20.2; Tacitus, *Annals*, 12.43). See also Sproul, *Last Days*, 40–41.

4. Sproul, *Last Days*, 43.

5. When Paul stated that the gospel had already reached the "whole world," he was writing around AD 58, which is likely when the letter to the Colossians was written. Robinson, *Redating*, 84.

6. Mathison, *Postmillennialism*, 111–15.

7. See also Acts 11:28, "And one of them named Agabus stood up and foretold by the Spirit that there would be a great famine over all the world [οἰκουμένη] (this took place in the days of Claudius)." Here, "all the world" refers to the Roman Empire, not the entire planet. Similarly, in Acts 24:5, it says, "For we have found this man a plague, one who stirs up riots among all the Jews throughout the world [οἰκουμένη] and is a ringleader of

Second, the phrase "all the nations" (ἔθνος, *ethnos*) in Matt 24:14 is interpreted to mean the various people groups within the Roman Empire, rather than nation-states, indicating a mandate to reach the diverse population under Roman rule.[8] Not only is this supported by the use of οἰκουμένη in the New Testament, as mentioned above, but also by the New Testament's focus of spreading the gospel to the gentiles (e.g., Acts 10:45; 11:18; Rom 1:5). Thus, "all the nations" supports the interpretation that the gospel was spread throughout the known world of the empire in the first century.

Third, Mathison notes that the primary audience for the gospel witness was the Jews scattered throughout the empire.[9] The extensive Jewish diaspora facilitated the spread of the gospel, as Jews living in various cities were familiar with the Hebrew Scriptures. Acts 21:21 highlights Jewish believers among the gentiles, indicating that the message of Jesus reached the dispersed Jews.[10] Similarly, Acts 24:5 describes Paul as causing disturbances among Jews throughout the empire, demonstrating the widespread influence of the gospel. Early Christian apologists even used the fulfillment of Jesus' prophecy as a key argument in their defense of Christianity.[11]

Fourth, the prophecy in Matt 24:14 speaks of a worldwide witness, not necessarily a worldwide conversion. The text specifies that the gospel will be "proclaimed" (κηρύσσω, *kerysso*) as a "testimony" (μαρτύριον, *martyrion*) to all nations, emphasizing the act of announcing or heralding the gospel rather than guaranteeing a universal conversion. The Greek verb κηρύσσω used here means to announce or herald, and the noun μαρτύριον signifies a witness or evidence given in a formal context.[12] The focus, then,

---

the sect of the Nazarenes." Again, "the world" in this context means the Roman Empire. Mathison, *Postmillennialism*, 112. See also Gentry, *Olivet Discourse*, 81–85; cf. Danker et al., *Lexicon*, 699.

8. Mathison, *Postmillennialism*, 113; Sproul, *Matthew*, 643–44; cf. Danker et al., *Lexicon*, 276.

9. Mathison, *Postmillennialism*, 113.

10. Sproul observes that during this period in the book of Acts, the Jewish Christians were numerous, with their numbers reaching into the thousands. Sproul, *Acts*, 322–23; cf. R. J. Knowling, "The Acts of the Apostles," in Nicoll, *Expositor's Greek Testament*, 2:449.

11. Origen argued that the specific and detailed nature of Jesus' predictions, including the fall of Jerusalem, could not have been mere coincidence but rather proof of his prophetic and divine insight (*Contra Celsum*, 2.13). Eusebius directly connects the destruction of Jerusalem with Jesus' prophecy. He interprets the event as a fulfillment of Jesus' words and a divine judgment against the Jews for rejecting him (*Church History*, 3.7).

12. In Mark 1:14, the word κηρύσσω is used to describe Jesus' act of announcing or

is on providing proof or a formal declaration of the gospel's truth and the coming kingdom, rather than the outcome of that witness.

Fifth, the fulfillment of this gospel mission is documented within the New Testament itself. The mission began in Acts 2 with Peter's sermon at Pentecost, addressing Jews from across the Roman Empire.[13] Acts 2:5 describes how "there were dwelling in Jerusalem Jews, devout men from every nation under heaven." This diverse assembly of Jewish diaspora, gathered for the Feast of Weeks, represented the breadth of the known world.[14] The Holy Spirit's outpouring enabled the apostles to speak in various languages which indicates the universal reach of the gospel.[15] Peter's sermon, therefore, marked the commencement of the gospel's dissemination to a global audience. As these Jews returned to their respective lands, they carried the message of the gospel with them, initiating the fulfillment of Jesus' prophecy: "This gospel of the kingdom will be proclaimed throughout the whole world" (Matt 24:14).

The apostle Paul offers clear evidence of the widespread dissemination of the gospel. In Rom 10:18, he references Ps 19:4, stating, "Their voice has gone out to all the earth, and their words to the ends of the world." This demonstrates Paul's conviction that the gospel had reached even the farthest reaches of the known world.[16] Furthermore, in Col 1:6 and 23,

---

heralding the good news of God's kingdom. In Acts 4:33, the term μαρτύριον is used to describe the apostles' witness to Jesus' resurrection. See also Danker et al., *Lexicon*, 543, 619.

13. Mathison, *Postmillennialism*, 113.

14. F. F. Bruce highlights the significance of the three major pilgrimage festivals observed during the first century AD. These festivals were timed around key points in the agricultural calendar: the seven-day Feast of Unleavened Bread, which began with the Passover feast around the spring equinox; Pentecost, occurring seven weeks later; and the Feast of Tabernacles, taking place around the autumn equinox. During these festivals, Jerusalem drew a significant number of Jews from diverse regions, along with some proselytes and devout gentiles, as mentioned in Acts 2:10. Bruce, *New Testament History*, 139–41.

15. Keener contrasts past interpretations linking speaking in tongues to incoherent speech in other cultures with contemporary views. He emphasizes Luke's portrayal of tongues as worship in unfamiliar languages, rooted in the Old Testament and connected to prophecy. This aligns with Luke's broader theme of inclusive, Spirit-inspired cross-cultural communication. Keener, *Background Commentary*, 322.

16. Sproul notes that God spread his gospel from Israel to the gentiles, aiming to stir jealousy among the Israelites (Rom 10:19). This aligns with God's promise to make Israel envious by sharing blessings with all nations (Deut 32:21). Paul emphasizes the universal proclamation of the gospel, emphasizing salvation for all who call upon the Lord's name

Paul reinforces this notion, affirming that the gospel had indeed spread throughout the known world, aligning with the prophecy of Matt 24:14 as interpreted in its historical context.

Abomination of Desolation

Considerable debate surrounds the "abomination of desolation" referenced in Matt 24:15. Futurists assert that this event is still forthcoming, while preterists argue that Jesus' prophesied event took place in the first century AD.[17] The following passage in the Olivet Discourse specifically addresses the abomination of desolation:

> So when you see the abomination of desolation spoken of by the prophet Daniel, standing in the holy place (let the reader understand), then let those who are in Judea flee to the mountains. Let the one who is on the housetop not go down to take what is in his house, and let the one who is in the field not turn back to take his cloak. And alas for women who are pregnant and for those who are nursing infants in those days! Pray that your flight may not be in winter or on a Sabbath. For then there will be great tribulation, such as has not been from the beginning of the world until now, no, and never will be. And if those days had not been cut short, no human being would be saved. But for the sake of the elect those days will be cut short. (Matt 24:15–22)

This study adopts a preterist perspective, contending that Jesus referred to a historical event to predict a similar one that would happen soon.[18] To begin, it is important to consider the Old Testament foundations and the historical context of Jesus' prophecy. Jay Rogers identifies four references in the book of Daniel pertinent to the abomination that causes desolation: Dan 8:13 and Dan 11:31 depict the defilement of the temple by Antiochus

---

(Rom 10:13). Sproul, *Romans*, 324–25.

17. Walvoord, *Prophecy*, 387–88; MacArthur, *Matthew 24-28*, 33–37; Gentry, *Olivet Discourse*, 87–94; Storms, *Kingdom Come*, 245–49.

18. The preterist interpretation of the abomination of desolation is not new in church history. Martin Luther, for instance, believed it occurred when Emperor Cajus, i.e., Caligula, placed his image in the Jerusalem temple for worship. He also connected verse 22 to the Roman-Jewish war in AD 68 to 70, suggesting that the suffering would be brief, as the conflict lasted less than two years before peace was declared. Luther, "Twenty-Fifth Sunday," 5:366–68. See also DeMar and Gumerlock, *New Testament Eschatology*, 104; Sproul, *Last Days*, 45–48.

Epiphanes from 168 to 165 BC. Likewise, Dan 9:27 and Dan 12:11 are associated with the devastation of the Second Temple by Roman forces under Vespasian and Titus during the Jewish-Roman War (AD 67–70).[19] These episodes involved the cessation of temple sacrifices due to the presence of pagan armies and idols within the consecrated precincts (the holy of holies).

The sacrilege perpetrated by Antiochus Epiphanes serves as a prototype for the events of the first century. Antiochus's actions, including the building of a pagan altar in the temple, suspended temple sacrifices for approximately three years. This historical event left a permanent mark on Jewish consciousness as an extreme act of blasphemy.[20] Similarly, Jesus' allusion in Matt 24:15 to the "abomination of desolation" draws upon this historical precedent. The Roman siege of Jerusalem and the subsequent destruction of the temple in AD 70 echoed the earlier desecration by Antiochus. Roman legions, under the command of Vespasian and his son Titus, breached the sacred precincts, resulting in another cessation of temple sacrifices and the ultimate annihilation of the Second Temple.[21]

Jesus taught that this event would pertain to the Second Temple and Jerusalem, rather than the entire world. It is, therefore, necessary to examine the context of Matt 24, using Gentry's argumentation as a basis for this discussion.[22] First, Jesus delivers these prophetic pronouncements while the temple stands in the "holy city," namely Jerusalem (Matt 4:5; 27:53). Second, Jesus' discourse is prompted by the disciples' observations concerning that specific temple in Jerusalem (23:38—24:3). Third, Jesus speaks of the impending destruction involving that temple (24:2). Fourth, Jesus instructs the disciples to "flee" (24:16). As Gentry notes, "If this were a worldwide event flight would not help."[23] Fifth, Jesus believed that flight

---

19. John Walvoord, a dispensationalist, also suggests that Dan 11:31 refers to the desecration of the temple by Antiochus Epiphanes. However, he sees the prophecy of Dan 9 as still future. In response, George L. Murray states, "The closing verse of Daniel nine has long been a stronghold for dispensationalism. Here, it is alleged, the angel describes and predicts the coming of Antichrist. Instead of reading out of the passage what it contains, the tendency is to read into it what some people think it ought to teach." Walvoord, *Prophecy*, 257, 387; Murray, *Millennial Studies*, 103.

20. For more information, see Dodd, "Fall of Jerusalem," 47–54, esp. 53; Ellis, *End of the World*, 32–35.

21. Rogers, *Prophecy of Daniel*, 35.

22. Gentry, *Olivet Discourse*, 87–94.

23. Gentry, *Olivet Discourse*, 92.

from the area would ensure their safety (24:17–20), implying the localized nature of his prophecy.

Historically, the flight of Christians from the city occurred prior to the final siege during an unforeseen and temporary withdrawal of the Roman legions. Historical accounts corroborate that many of these Christians sought refuge in the rock fortress of Pella, situated approximately sixty miles northeast of Jerusalem.[24] Thus, the historical context and the coherent progression of the passage and its surroundings unequivocally suggest that the "abomination of desolation" referenced the Roman siege of Jerusalem and the ensuing destruction of the temple, which mirrored the earlier desecration by Antiochus Epiphanes.

De-Creation Language

The passage from Matt 24:15–35 has long been a focal point for discussions on eschatology, particularly regarding the end of the world. Verses 29–30 have prompted significant debate regarding the details of this great tribulation:

> Immediately after the tribulation of those days the sun will be darkened, and the moon will not give its light, and the stars will fall from heaven, and the powers of the heavens will be shaken. Then will appear in heaven the sign of the Son of Man, and then all the tribes of the earth will mourn, and they will see the Son of Man coming on the clouds of heaven with power and great glory. (Matt 24:29–30)

The futurist interpretation, which takes a literal approach to these verses, posits that these events must refer to a future occurrence, as the galaxy has not yet been destroyed.[25] However, this kind of de-creation language is often found within the Old Testament to signify the destruction of a city or nation.[26]

---

24. DeMar and Gumerlock, *New Testament Eschatology*, 115; Mathison, *Postmillennialism*, 113.

25. William MacDonald writes, "The stars will plunge from heaven, and planets will be moved out of their orbits." Likewise, Walvoord states, "The Second Coming will be preceded by many supernatural events in the skies." MacDonald, *Believer's Bible Commentary*, 1218; Walvoord, *Prophecy*, 389.

26. Chilton, *Paradise Restored*, 98–100; Gentry, *He Shall Have Dominion*, 356.

For instance, Isa 13:10 describes God's judgment on Babylon: "For the stars of the heavens and their constellations will not give their light; the sun will be dark at its rising, and the moon will not shed its light." Similarly, Isa 34:4, concerning the destruction of Bozrah in Edom, states, "All the host of heaven shall rot away, and the skies roll up like a scroll. All their host shall fall, as leaves fall from the vine, like leaves falling from the fig tree." Ezekiel 32:7, in lamentation over Pharaoh, declares, "When I blot you out, I will cover the heavens and make their stars dark; I will cover the sun with a cloud, and the moon shall not give its light." Thus, when Jesus employs similar language in Matt 24, it should be understood as an allusion to Old Testament prophetic symbolism rather than a prediction of literal astronomical events (cf. Joel 2:10, 31; Amos 8:9). This interpretation is further supported by the immediate context of Jesus' discourse, which focuses on the impending judgment upon Jerusalem (Matt 24:1–3).

Coming on the Clouds

The phrase "coming on the clouds" in Matt 24:30 does not necessarily refer to the second advent of Christ. While the present author affirms belief in the second coming of Christ (cf. Acts 1:11; 1 Thess 4:15–17), this phrase here is better understood as a metaphor for divine judgment, drawing from Old Testament imagery. For example, Pss 18:7–15 and 104:3, Isa 19:1, and Joel 2:1–2 all utilize cloud imagery to depict God's presence and judgment. Revelation 1:7 echoes this theme, reinforcing the interpretation that Jesus' reference to coming on the clouds pertains to his judgment upon Israel in the first century, particularly those responsible for his crucifixion (see chapter 6 for more information regarding the theme of Revelation).[27] In essence, both the Olivet Discourse and Revelation address the destruction of Jerusalem and the Second Temple (see the context, Matt 24:1–3).

Parable of the Fig Tree

In Matt 24:32–35, the parable of the fig tree serves to illustrate the time frame for Jerusalem's destruction. Jesus states in verse 34, "Truly, I say to you, this generation will not pass away until all these things take place."

---

27. Gentry also examines the theme of the book of Revelation, illustrating how the cloud imagery correlates with the destruction of Jerusalem and the Second Temple. Gentry, *Before Jerusalem Fell*, 121–32. See also Quintern, "Neronic Date," 77–83.

The term "this generation" (γενεά, *genea*) has been a point of contention, with some arguing it refers to the entirety of believers throughout the ages.[28] However, this interpretation deviates from the primary meaning of "generation" in the New Testament, which typically denotes the contemporary audience of Jesus' time (cf. Matt 11:16; 12:39, 41–42, 45; 17:17).[29]

Mathison states, "The parable of the fig tree does not refer to the restoration of the nation of Israel in [AD] 1948. In the parallel passage in Luke 21:29, Jesus refers to 'the fig tree, and all the trees.' The point that Jesus is making is that when the disciples see these things beginning to occur, they should know that his coming in judgment upon Jerusalem is near."[30] In Jewish tradition, a "generation" spans approximately forty years, aligning with the period between Jesus' crucifixion around AD 30 and the destruction of Jerusalem and the Second Temple in AD 70.[31] Therefore, the term "this generation" in Matt 24:34 likely refers to Christ's contemporaries, particularly the Jews who rejected him.

MacArthur argues that the phrase "let the reader understand" (v. 15) indicates that Jesus intended his warnings and the Olivet Discourse, not for the disciples or their contemporaries, but for believers in the future. By reading his warnings in Scripture, MacArthur argues, the future believers will gain understanding of the challenges they will face.[32] However, the phrase "let the reader understand" does not imply a distant future fulfillment. Instead, it likely served as a practical admonition for the contemporary readers of the Gospel of Matthew to recognize and respond to the coming signs of judgment on Jerusalem. Jesus spoke prior to his crucifixion in AD 30, and Matthew wrote his Gospel likely before AD 62.[33] Thus, there would be a clear sense of urgency intended by Matthew to his contemporaries.

The parallel accounts in Mark 13 and Luke 21 also highlight the urgency of these events. Luke 21:20, for example, specifies that the abomination of desolation refers to Jerusalem being surrounded by armies: "But

---

28. David Hill contends that since Jesus states that he does not know the day or hour, the term "generation" cannot apply to Jesus' contemporary audience. Sproul responds that it is possible to predict an event within the next forty years while recognizing uncertainty about its specific timing within that time frame. Hill, *Gospel of Matthew*, 323; Sproul, *Last Days*, 58–59.

29. Russell, *Parousia*, 84–89; Sproul, *Last Days*, 68–71.

30. Mathison, *Postmillennialism*, 114–15.

31. Gentry, *He Shall Have Dominion*, 350–51; Sproul, *Last Days*, 64.

32. MacArthur, *Matthew 24–28*, 37.

33. Robinson, *Redating*, 107.

when you see Jerusalem surrounded by armies, then know that its desolation has come near." This served as a clear signal for first-century Christians to flee the city, which they historically did by escaping to Pella, as mentioned above. The early Christians, primarily Jewish and living in or around Jerusalem, would have seen Jesus' warnings as immediately relevant.

SUMMARY

This chapter, while not exhaustive, has reassessed the Olivet Discourse, arguing that it primarily pertains to the destruction of Jerusalem and the Second Temple, rather than signaling a future global tribulation. The discourse begins with Jesus predicting the temple's destruction, and he continues by cautioning the disciples about false messiahs, wars, famines, and earthquakes. The phrase "the whole world" in Matt 24:14, often interpreted as requiring the gospel's proclamation to every individual globally, is reexamined within its historical context, indicating the Roman Empire.

The "abomination of desolation" is explored through a preterist lens, drawing parallels between the historical desecration by Antiochus Epiphanes and the Roman siege of Jerusalem in AD 70. This historical event is contextualized within the narrative of Matt 24, emphasizing its localized nature. Moreover, the parable of the fig tree, specifically the term "this generation," is examined within the context of first-century Jews, suggesting that Jesus' prophecy was meant for his contemporaries. Overall, this chapter has offered an interpretation of the Olivet Discourse that aligns with historical events, supporting the postmillennial view by demonstrating that the "great tribulation" is a past event, fulfilled through the destruction of Jerusalem and the Second Temple.

Chapter Six

Contextual Foundations of Revelation

AUTHORSHIP

In the text of Revelation, the author explicitly identifies himself as John on four occasions (Rev 1:1, 4, 9; 22:8). However, the narrative does not furnish any supplementary designations for this figure. Notably absent are any honorific titles or alternative names, and the author refrains from asserting any familial proximity to Jesus or prominence within the early Christian community.[1]

Traditionally, the apostle John is credited with the authorship of Revelation. However, the name John was common in the early Christian era, leaving the identity of this particular John open to question.[2] Leonard L. Thompson suggests that this John might have been an early Christian prophet who traveled through the churches of Asia Minor, either on random journeys or following a predetermined route.[3]

In his commentary on Revelation, Gentry, affirming apostolic authorship, offers several points challenging the notion of Johannine authorship as an absolute necessity for the divine inspiration status of the text. First, he

---

1. Thomas and Macchia, *Revelation*, 36.

2. Richard Bauckham provides a detailed analysis of naming conventions in first-century Palestine. His findings indicate that the name John (*Yohanan*) was among the top six most common male names of the period. Bauckham, *Jesus and the Eyewitnesses*, 76.

3. Thompson notes that the role of prophets in the early church is well-documented and highly esteemed. Paul accords it significant importance, ranking it second only to apostleship (1 Cor 12:28). Additionally, it is often linked with the office of teaching (cf. Acts 13:1). The *Didache*, an early Christian document, describes prophets as itinerant ministers, providing guidelines for their reception and support in chapters 11–13. Thompson, *Book of Revelation*, 12.

contends that there is no compelling inspirational imperative for attributing the authorship to the apostle John. While the text identifies the author as being named John, it does not explicitly claim apostolic authorship.[4] Second, Gentry argues against a theological compulsion for Johannine authorship, asserting that the canonicity of Revelation does not hinge on apostolic attribution according to Scripture. He posits that the inclusion of books in the Christian canon derives from their inherent divine inspiration (cf. 2 Tim 3:16; 1 Thess 2:13), rather than from contemporary attempts to ascertain authorship. Third, he dismisses any exegetical necessity for Johannine authorship, suggesting that the interpretation of the text remains unaffected by uncertainty surrounding the author's identity.[5]

External Evidence

While identifying the author of Revelation is not mandatory for its canonical status, the external evidence strongly supports the claim that the book was written by the apostle John. Early church fathers such as Justin Martyr (ca. AD 100–165), Irenaeus (ca. AD 120–202), Tertullian (ca. AD 160–220), Hippolytus (ca. AD 170–236), and Origen (ca. AD 195–253) affirm John's authorship directly.[6] However, there are early sources that challenge this view. Notably, Dionysius of Alexandria (ca. AD 200–265) and Eusebius (ca. AD 260–340) oppose the apostolic authorship of Revelation.

Dionysius argued that the varying styles among Revelation, the Fourth Gospel, and the Epistles of John implied distinct authors, casting doubt on the notion that Revelation was composed by the same person.[7] While considering the possibility of John Mark as being the author, he dismissed it due to Mark not being mentioned in Acts as traveling to Asia Minor. Alternatively, he proposed the existence of a second John, supported by the presence of two tombs in Ephesus believed to belong to individuals named John.[8]

Eusebius identified the writer through the tradition of Papias of Hierapolis (ca. AD 60–130). However, Stephen S. Smalley raises doubts regarding whether Papias indeed referenced two distinct disciples named John,

---

4. Gentry, *Divorce of Israel*, 1:12.
5. Gentry, *Divorce of Israel*, 1:13.
6. Terry, *Apocalypse of John*, 1.
7. Guthrie, *Introduction*, 933.
8. Guthrie, *Introduction*, 934.

one designated as "the elder." Smalley suggests it is more plausible that Papias was referring to the same John, the apostle, in two different contexts: first, among deceased disciples of Jesus, and second, among those still living.[9] In both instances, "elder" signifies "seniority in the faith." Hence, when "elder" appears alongside John's name in its subsequent occurrence, it likely denotes John the apostle's status rather than indicating another individual.[10] Even Eusebius acknowledges that Papias described the apostles as "elders."[11]

Internal Evidence

Although the book does not explicitly claim authorship by the apostle John or provide any direct evidence to support this assertion, there are internal factors that strongly suggest he might indeed be the author. First, historical association links John the apostle with the churches in Asia Minor, where the book's messages are directed.[12] Second, the author of Revelation displays a keen awareness of the significance of his role, conveying a sense of authority that seems widely respected.[13] Third, while Revelation falls within the apocalyptic genre, it diverges from Jewish conventions by not attributing itself to ancient figures like Enoch or Ezra.[14]

Moreover, those who assert that the apostle John wrote both the Gospel of John and the book of Revelation point to similarities between the two texts to support their claim of shared authorship.[15] They argue that any differences in literary style can be attributed to the distinct genres of

---

9. Smalley, *Thunder and Love*, 38.

10. Smalley, *Thunder and Love*, 38.

11. Eusebius, *Church History*, 3.39.7. The evidence regarding Papias's views on the identity of the apostle John, the supposed author of Revelation, is primarily indirect. Consequently, it remains uncertain whether Papias attributed the authorship of Revelation to John or not. Koester, *Revelation*, 66.

12. Gentry, *Divorce of Israel*, 1:15; Guthrie, *Introduction*, 935.

13. Gentry, *Divorce of Israel*, 1:15.

14. Guthrie notes that the author prophesies in his own name, implying a departure from tradition likely fueled by a belief in the renewed activity of prophetic spirit, rendering pseudonymous attribution unnecessary. Guthrie, *Introduction*, 935. For more information related to apocalyptic pseudonymity, see Rowland, *Open Heaven*, 69.

15. For more detailed information on the similarities in vocabulary, syntax, and theological themes between the Gospel of John and the book of Revelation, see Reynolds, *John among the Apocalypses*, 167–99.

the works.[16] Since Revelation is a different genre from the Fourth Gospel, variations in literary aspects between the two texts are to be expected.

COMPOSITION DATE

C. Marvin Pate rightly observes that understanding the date and historical context of Revelation is crucial for its interpretation.[17] The contention over the dating of Revelation revolves around two primary dates of composition: the Neronic date (AD 64–68) and the Domitianic date (AD 95–96). Advocates of the early date, such as Gentry, argue for a pre-AD 70 composition. Conversely, defenders of the Domitianic date, like Mark L. Hitchcock, propose a later time frame. This section will focus on the internal evidence supporting the early date, particularly concerning the identification of the beast in Revelation.[18]

Beast of Revelation

A key element in identifying Revelation's date lies in interpreting the symbolic language used to describe the beast. Revelation portrays the beast with seven heads, a characteristic often interpreted to represent the succession of Roman emperors. This interpretation finds support in Rev 17:9–10, where an angel explains that the seven heads symbolize seven kings, five of whom have fallen, one who is, and one who is yet to come. John describes the beast with seven heads (Rev 13:1), suggesting a collective identity. Later, the beast is linked to the number 666 (13:18), implying a specific individualistic identity. Scholars generally agree on this dual nature of the beast in Revelation, representing both a kingdom and a king.[19]

---

16. Koester, *Revelation*, 66.

17. Pate, *Interpreting*, 137–38.

18. While external evidence is important in dating texts, the external evidence for the date of the book of Revelation is inconclusive. The primary sources supporting a late date often merely echo earlier opinions, while others are divided, some favoring a later date and others an earlier one. Gentry argues convincingly for the early date, countered by Hitchcock who refutes Gentry's points. This present author, in his dissertation, defends Gentry's position against Hitchcock's objections. Interested readers should consult these works for more information on the date of Revelation, specifically information related to external sources. Gentry, *Before Jerusalem Fell*; Quintern, "Neronic Date"; Hitchcock, "Domitianic Date."

19. Gentry, *Beast of Revelation*, 10–11. See also Aune, *Revelation 17–22*, 944–45;

Smalley emphasizes the significance of Rome's seven hills in understanding the symbolism. Rome was famously known as the City of Seven Hills, making the connection between the heads and Roman emperors evident to contemporary readers.[20] In the same way that New York is often called the Big Apple, Wilson notes, Rome was known as the city of seven hills, and the first-century reader would probably have recognized this allusion.[21] Therefore, this study contends that Rome represents the beast's collective identity while Nero Caesar represents the beast's specific identity. Argumentation to identify Nero as the beast will follow.

Line of Kings

Revelation 17:9–10 states, "This calls for a mind with wisdom: the seven heads are seven mountains on which the woman is seated; they are also seven kings, five of whom have fallen, one is, the other has not yet come, and when he does come he must remain only a little while." To establish the time frame, it is essential to identify the emperors referenced by the five fallen heads and the one reigning during the composition of Revelation. Adela Y. Collins highlights the author's real-time calculation, suggesting that it has a meaningful historical context.[22] The list of emperors, starting with Julius Caesar, aligns with the count in Revelation, identifying Nero Caesar as the sixth king reigning at the time the text was written.[23]

Despite some debate regarding the starting point of the emperor count, evidence from historians like Suetonius[24] and Dio Cassius[25] supports Julius Caesar's inclusion as the first emperor.[26] Moreover, Josephus, a first-century Jewish historian contemporaneous with the author of Revelation, places Augustus as the second emperor, indicating Julius Caesar as

---

Swete, *Apocalypse of St. John*, 220.

20. Smalley, *Revelation to John*, 435.

21. Wilson, *Commentary*, 148–49.

22. Collins, "Dating the Apocalypse," 36.

23. The most logical enumeration of the Roman emperors appears to be as follows: Julius Caesar (49–44 BC), Augustus (31 BC–AD 14), Tiberius (AD 14–37), Gaius, also known as Caligula (AD 37–41), Claudius (AD 41–54), Nero (AD 54–68), Galba (AD 68–69), Otho (AD 69), Vitellius (AD 69), and Vespasian (AD 69–79).

24. Suetonius, *Julius*, 76.

25. Dio Cassius, Roman History, 5, noted in Gentry, Before Jerusalem Fell, 155.

26. For more information regarding the line of kings, see Beckwith, *Apocalypse of John*, 704–8; Gentry, *Before Jerusalem Fell*, 151–64; Quintern, "Neronic Date," 91–98.

the first.[27] This aligns with the interpretation that Nero, reigning during Revelation's composition, corresponds to the sixth head of the beast.

Number of the Beast

Revelation 13:18 states, "This calls for wisdom: let the one who has understanding calculate the number of the beast, for it is the number of a man, and his number is 666." The directive to "calculate the number of the beast" implies that the prophecies were relevant to the first century, as John assumed his readers could identify the beast in their historical context. Preterists tend to interpret the number 666 as a cryptogram pointing to Nero Caesar.[28] This interpretation is reinforced by a textual variant in Rev 13:18, presenting the numerical value of 616, which also aligns with Nero's name through alternative spellings.

Craig R. Koester notes that while the Greek letters for Nero (transliterated as "Neron") total 1005, the Hebrew letters (נרון קסר) total 666.[29] The textual variant 616 aligns with the Latin spelling "Nero," showing a deliberate adaptation for different linguistic contexts. Bruce M. Metzger supports this, noting that "Neron Caesar" in Hebrew equals 666, and "Nero Caesar" equals 616.[30] Furthermore, the Greek word for "beast" (θηρίον, *thērion*) in Hebrew letters also totals 666, suggesting a connection between the beast and Nero.[31] Thus, the evidence of both 666 and 616 as numerical values pointing to Nero Caesar, combined with historical and linguistic considerations, supports the interpretation of Nero as the beast of Revelation.[32]

---

27. Josephus, *Antiquities*, 18:2:2.

28. Cryptograms, or *gematria*, were not exclusive to Jewish and Christian traditions; they were used in various ancient cultures. An interesting example of this can be seen on the walls of certain Pompeii ruins, where a graffiti message reads, "I love her whose number is 545." Bahnsen, *Victory in Jesus*, 21; Gentry, *Beast of Revelation*, 41–43; Hillegonds, *Early Date*, 139–41; Mathison, *Postmillennialism*, 145; Sproul, *Last Days*, 202–4.

29. Koester, "Number of the Beast," 9.

30. Francis X. Gumerlock cites early references linking Nero with the number 616, indicating an ancient recognition of this association. Gumerlock, "Nero Antichrist," 358–60; Metzger, *Textual Commentary*, 750.

31. Koester, "Number of the Beast," 9.

32. For a more detailed examination of the number of the beast, including responses to objections, see Quintern, "Neronic Date," 98–105.

Audience Relevance

In understanding ancient texts like the Bible, it is essential to grasp the audience the author had in mind. Gentry notes that evangelical scholars commonly use the grammatical-historical method of interpretation, which entails analyzing passages in their historical and contemporary contexts (see chapter 2).[33] This approach is useful for understanding the message of Revelation, given its historical audience.

John, when composing Revelation, tailored his message to specific church communities, as evident from the letter's recipients: the congregations in Ephesus, Smyrna, Pergamum, Thyatira, Sardis, Philadelphia, and Laodicea (Rev 1:10–11). The order of these cities matches a Roman courier route, highlighting the practical communication methods of the time.[34] Essentially, John addressed real churches in Asia Minor during the first century, considering each community's unique historical context.[35] In short, John was not predicting distant events but addressing immediate challenges faced by persecuted first-century Christians (Rev 1:3).

Temporal Expectation

The text consistently emphasizes the imminence of various prophecies, referring to them as "at hand" or "soon to take place" (Rev 1:1; 22:6). This sense of urgency throughout the letter suggests that John anticipated the rapid fulfillment of these prophecies shortly after writing. Notably, the introduction (1:1, 3, 19) and conclusion (22:6, 7, 12, 20) contain instances of contemporary expectation, indicating John's consistent emphasis on the imminent nature of these events. Gentry observes that the strategic placement of these prophecies within the introductory and concluding chapters highlights their significance.[36] Furthermore, John employs two distinct

---

33. Similarly, Gordon D. Fee and Douglas Stuart highlight the importance of understanding the original intent, historical backdrop, literary setting, and significance of the material. The objective is to discern the author's purpose in composing a specific text by delving into the historical context in which they and their initial audience lived. Fee and Stuart, *How to Read the Bible*, 27–35; Gentry, *Divorce of Israel*, 1:45. See also Schökel, *Manual of Hermeneutics*, 16.

34. Ramsay, *Letters to the Seven*, 186.

35. For more information, see Gentry, *Perilous Times*, 122–23. Quintern, "Neronic Date," 84.

36. Gentry, *Before Jerusalem Fell*, 133.

Greek terms, τάχος (*tachos*) and ἐγγύς (*eggus*),³⁷ to convey his expectation of their near fulfillment.³⁸ In essence, the precise choice of language by John leaves little room for debate regarding his expectation that these events would occur shortly, rather than being deferred thousands of years into the future.

Neronic Persecution

In the introduction to Revelation, John speaks of his own exile, indicating that the book was likely written during a time of severe Christian persecution (Rev 1:9).³⁹ This period coincides with the onset of persecution triggered by the fire in Rome (AD 64), which Nero unjustly blamed on the Christians, setting the stage for the events depicted in Revelation.⁴⁰ Nero, notorious for his cruelty and debauchery, as recorded by historians like Suetonius, engaged in actions reminiscent of the tyrannical figure portrayed in Revelation.

His barbaric treatment of Christians, including forcing them to fight in arenas, and his self-indulgent lifestyle mirror the malevolent characteristics associated with the beast (13:5–10).⁴¹ For instance, Nero's insistence on being worshipped and his relentless persecution of Christians align with the beast's description (13:4–15; 14:9–11; 16:2; 19:20; 20:4).⁴² Additionally,

---

37. The term "*tachos*" means a "very brief amount of time," and the term "*eggus*" means "being close in point of time, near." Danker et al., *Lexicon*, 992, 241.

38. Gentry notes that nearly every modern English translation of the Bible uses language that describes something that would come in a short period of time. Considering John's use of the Greek language, one should assume that he anticipated that these developments would occur soon, and likely within his own lifetime. Gentry, *Perilous Times*, 124–25.

39. Beckwith, *Apocalypse of John*, 208–13.

40. Baur, *Church History*, 2:192; Wilson, *Commentary*, 151–52.

41. Further evil actions of Nero also include the vicious murder of his pregnant wife, orchestrating the killings of family members, and even engaging in grotesque acts like castrating a young boy whom he later treated as his spouse. He also burned Christians at the stake to illuminate his gardens as he strolled through them. Suetonius, *Nero*, 16, 26, 28–29, 33–35; Gentry, *Beast of Revelation*, 14–17. See also Shelley and Shelley, *Church History*, 52–53.

42. Leon Morris recognizes that beginning with Nero's reign, the cult of the Roman Emperor progressively gained reverence, suggesting that the references in Revelation may be applicable to the era during or after Nero. Moreover, Robinson notes that Nero had a statue of himself in Rome, designed for worship, that was the same size as the statue

the duration of Nero's persecution, roughly forty-two months, remarkably corresponds to the time frame mentioned in Rev 13:5: "And the beast was given a mouth uttering haughty and blasphemous words, and it was allowed to exercise authority for forty-two months." This alignment strengthens the argument identifying Nero as the persecutor described in the text. Thus, considering the historical context, Nero's personality traits, and the duration of his persecution, all evidence points to him as the bestial figure of persecution depicted in the book of Revelation.

CULTURAL CONTEXT OF REVELATION

Understanding the cultural backdrop of the Roman Empire is crucial for interpreting the book of Revelation, especially the sociopolitical and economic conditions in first-century Jerusalem. This historical setting sheds light on how power dynamics, religious practices, and economic factors shaped the experiences of early Christians. This section will briefly address the Herodian dynasty, the imperial cult, and the economic environment of the time.

Herodian Dynasty

Herod the Great was appointed king of Judea by the Roman senate in 37 BC, despite being of Idumean (Edomite) descent, which caused tension among many Jews who questioned his legitimacy.[43] Herod undertook extensive construction projects, notably renovating the Jerusalem temple, which became one of the most magnificent structures of its time. However, his harsh rule and executions alienated much of the Jewish population. His strong alliance with Rome brought political support but also enforced unpopular Roman policies and taxes, contributing to the Jewish resistance and the Great Jewish Revolt of AD 66–70.

---

of Mars. Morris, *Revelation of St. John*, 35; Robinson, *Redating*, 236; Quintern, "Neronic Date," 112.

43. The Edomites possibly supported Babylonian forces in the ca. 586 BC destruction of Jerusalem, fostering long-standing animosity from the Jewish community (Ps 137:7). This hostility traces back to Edom's ancient refusal to allow Moses passage through their territory (Num 20:18–21). John Hyrcanus later (134–104 BC) forced the Idumeans to convert to Judaism, including undergoing circumcision. Grant, *Herod the Great*, 20–21. See also Josephus, *Antiquities*, 4.15.2.

Herod Agrippa I, grandson of Herod the Great, was educated in Rome and maintained close ties with Roman emperors, notably Caligula, who granted him territories and the title of king.[44] Attempting to gain favor with the Jews, Agrippa I executed James, the brother of John, and imprisoned Peter (Acts 12). Agrippa I's violent death in AD 44 is recorded in both Acts 12:20–23 and by Josephus.[45]

Herod Agrippa II, son of Agrippa I, ruled over Chalcis and later inherited territories north and east of the Sea of Galilee. He advised Roman officials on Jewish affairs and played a notable role during the Jewish revolt of AD 66. Agrippa II is remembered for hearing Paul's defense and for his support of Rome during the revolt (Acts 26:1–2). After his death around AD 92, his territories were absorbed into the Roman province of Syria, ending the Herodian line.[46]

Following Agrippa I's death, Judea returned to the governance of Roman procurators like Felix and Festus, whose mismanagement and harsh policies contributed to mounting tensions that led to the Jewish revolt in AD 66 (cf. Acts 24–25). The revolt was initially successful for the Jews but was eventually quelled by Roman forces under Vespasian and his son Titus. The revolt culminated in the destruction of Jerusalem and the Second Temple in AD 70, marking a significant turning point in Jewish history.[47]

Understanding the Herodian dynasty is useful for interpreting Revelation as it offers important historical context regarding Judea's political and social landscape under Roman rule. The Herodian rulers' alliance with Rome, their authoritarian reign, and key events like the Jewish revolt and the fall of Jerusalem directly shaped early Christian communities. This background highlights Revelation's themes of persecution, martyrdom, political loyalty, and divine judgment, contributing to one's understanding of its symbolic language and prophetic messages (e.g., Rev 17:1–6, where the imagery of the harlot seated on the beast depicts Jerusalem's corrupt political power allied with Rome).[48]

---

44. Caligula ordered that a statue of himself should be erected in the Jerusalem temple, but it was never carried out due to Jewish resistance, Agrippa I's intervention, and Caligula's subsequent assassination. Josephus, *Antiquities*, 18.8.2.

45. Josephus, *Antiquities*, 19.8.2; Ferguson, *Backgrounds*, 413.

46. Ferguson, *Backgrounds*, 418–19.

47. Ferguson, *Backgrounds*, 419–23.

48. See chapter 7 for more information.

The Imperial Cult

The origins of the imperial cult can be traced back to the aftermath of Julius Caesar's assassination in 44 BC. Following Caesar's death, his heir Octavian (later Augustus) formed the Second Triumvirate alongside Mark Antony and Marcus Aemilius Lepidus, leading to the fall of the Roman Republic.[49] Octavian eventually defeated Antony, who had been deified by the province of Asia, and became the sole ruler of Rome after Antony's suicide alongside Cleopatra. In 29 BC, the elders of Asia requested permission to establish a cult in honor of Octavian, driven by political allegiance and genuine appreciation for the peace and prosperity he brought to the East.[50] This initiative marked the beginning of widespread enthusiasm for the imperial cult.

James S. McLaren highlights the evidence regarding interactions between Jews and the imperial cult in the first century. Most incidents occurred during Caligula's reign as he was "particularly active in promoting his divine status."[51] He notes that the imperial cult varied regionally due to the lack of an empire-wide mandate. Moreover, he notes Jewish reluctance towards images and cult participation, with conflicts arising in Alexandria, Jamnia, and Dora. Herod's support of the cult in Judea exemplifies early integration, but tensions persisted, especially after the temple's destruction in AD 70.[52]

Understanding the imperial cult is important for interpreting Revelation due to its impact on early Christians. Participation in emperor worship was crucial for societal acceptance, and refusal often resulted in ostracism, sanctions, and persecution.[53] Revelation's symbolic imagery frequently references the imperial cult; for example, the beast in Rev 13, demanding worship and blaspheming God, symbolizes Roman emperors and the imperial cult. Refusing the mark of the beast is a metaphor for rejecting emperor worship.

---

49. Nicholas Perrin, "The Imperial Cult," in Green and McDonald, *World of the New Testament*, 124–25.

50. Nicholas Perrin, "The Imperial Cult," in Green and McDonald, *World of the New Testament*, 125. See also Tacitus, *Annals*, 4.37.

51. McLaren, "Jews and the Imperial Cult," 274.

52. McLaren, "Jews and the Imperial Cult," 276–77.

53. Collins, "Dating the Apocalypse," 39. See also Shelley and Shelley, *Church History*, 55–57.

Economics

In the first century, the economy of Roman Judea was primarily based on agricultural production, with grain, olives, and grapes being the main crops. David J. Downs notes that the region's economic structure is often debated in terms of whether it should be considered as an "advanced agrarian society," which means that urban centers were in control of resources through mechanisms like rent, taxation, and limited trade by non-elites. However, evidence suggests there was significant regional trade in goods such as pottery and olive oil.[54]

Taxation and tribute were critical aspects of Roman control in Palestine. Downs notes that after Judea came under Roman rule in 63 BC, the Roman tribute was initially collected irregularly by tax collectors.[55] Under Herod the Great, various taxes—including the Roman tribute, the temple tax, and local levies—were collected. Scholars differ on the impact these taxes had on Jewish peasants, but it is clear that Herod's descendants likely enjoyed exemptions from Roman tribute due to their Roman citizenship.[56]

The transition to Roman provincial rule in AD 6 brought a renewed imposition of the tribute, accompanied by a census to facilitate taxation under Quirinius. This period saw significant resistance among Jews to the census and taxation policies, as reflected in biblical and historical accounts.[57] Jesus' response on paying taxes to Caesar illustrates the broader tensions over fiscal obligations and Roman authority (Matt 22:15–22). This background of taxation and agricultural dependency gives the reader more context for understanding the economic imagery depicted in the Apocalypse (cf. Rev 18:11–13).

GEOGRAPHICAL CONTEXT OF REVELATION

William B. Tolar observes that John's exile to Patmos becomes more understandable when viewed in its historical context (cf. Rev 1:9). Roman

---

54. David J. Downs, "Economics, Taxes, and Tithes," in Green and McDonald, *World of the New Testament*, 160–62.

55. David J. Downs, "Economics, Taxes, and Tithes," in Green and McDonald, *World of the New Testament*, 163.

56. David J. Downs, "Economics, Taxes, and Tithes," in Green and McDonald, *World of the New Testament*, 164.

57. David J. Downs, "Economics, Taxes, and Tithes," in Green and McDonald, *World of the New Testament*, 164.

historians, like Tacitus, indicate that first-century emperors used this small, rocky, volcanic island as a prison for criminals, who were tasked with quarrying rock.[58] Likewise, Tolar notes, comprehending the history, culture, and religious context of the seven cities addressed in Rev 2–3 strengthens one's understanding of the letters to the churches.[59] Therefore, this section will briefly present geographical information relevant to interpreting the book of Revelation.

The Island of Patmos

Charles F. Pfeiffer notes that Patmos is situated approximately seventy miles southwest of Ephesus. The island measures roughly twenty miles in circumference and spans an area of about fifty square miles. Known for its rocky and barren terrain, Patmos served as an ideal location for the exile of criminals due to its isolation.[60]

Ephesus

According to Thomas V. Brisco, Ephesus, situated on the western coast of Asia Minor, stood as a prominent commercial center renowned for its magnificent temple dedicated to Artemis, counted among the Seven Wonders of the Ancient World. As the capital of the prosperous province of Asia, Ephesus was notably associated with the apostle Paul, who resided there for over two years. The city boasted influential figures involved in the provincial assembly, tasked with promoting and enforcing the worship of the emperor.[61] Revelation 2:1–7 commends the Ephesian church for their works and endurance but warns against forsaking their initial love, implying a possible drift caused by external pressures.

---

58. Tacitus, *Annals*, 4.30.

59. William B. Tolar, "The Grammatical-Historical Method," in Corley et al., *Biblical Hermeneutics*, 36. For more information related to the seven churches of Asia, see Hemer, *Letters to the Seven Churches*.

60. Pfeiffer, *Baker's Bible Atlas*, 233.

61. Brisco, *Holman Bible Atlas*, 254

Smyrna

Smyrna, a flourishing harbor city with important trade routes reaching through the Hermus Valley to Sardis, was renowned for its beauty, referred to by ancient writers as one of the most beautiful cities in Ionia (modern-day Turkey).[62] Brisco observes that the city boasted broad, finely paved streets and was adorned with temples, baths, a stadium, and many other luxuries, serving a population of over one hundred thousand. The city was honored by Tiberius with the privilege of constructing an imperial temple for the imperial cult.[63] Polycarp, a disciple of the apostle John, was martyred in Smyrna's stadium.[64]

Pergamum

Pfeiffer notes that Pergamum, located sixty miles northeast of Smyrna, was the capital of a small kingdom that emerged after the fall of Alexander's empire. The city's significance is highlighted by its role in the defeat of Antiochus III at Magnesia, which is commemorated in the frieze of the great altar of Zeus in Pergamum.[65] This altar, featuring a statue of Zeus nearly fifty feet high in a colonnaded enclosure, is believed by some to be the "Satan's throne" mentioned in Rev 2:13.[66]

Interpretations of "Satan's throne" vary. According to Gentry, John Lightfoot suggests it refers to the unbelieving Jews, whom the Bible calls the "synagogue of Satan" (Rev 2:9). However, Gentry argues that it alludes to Rome's provincial headquarters in Pergamum, with its strong imperial cult, noting that the Jewish presence was likely not strong enough to justify this designation.[67] Craig S. Keener supports the view that "Satan's throne" refers to the local emperor worship, which was prominent on Pergamum's coinage and predated the Roman period. He notes that Pergamum was among

---

62. Strabo, *Geography*, 14.1.37.

63. Tacitus, *Annals*, 4.55–56.

64. *Martyrdom of Polycarp*, 15–19, in Ehrman, *Apostolic Fathers*, 357–403; Brisco, *Holman Bible Atlas*, 265.

65. Pfeiffer, *Baker's Bible Atlas*, 233.

66. Pfeiffer, *Baker's Bible Atlas*, 234.

67. Gentry, *Divorce of Israel*, 1:438–39.

the first cities in Asia to build a temple to a Roman emperor, dedicated to Augustus.⁶⁸

Thyatira

Thyatira, situated thirty five miles southeast of Pergamum, was a small city renowned for its textile trade. The city, notes Brisco, boasted various trade guilds, including bakers, potters, tanners, and coppersmiths, alongside a prominent textile industry. This industry, featuring wool merchants, dyers, and linen workers, gained particular prominence. Dyers, using a prized purple dye from the murex shell, catered to wealthy clientele, and Thyatira's export of purple cloth significantly bolstered its economy.⁶⁹

Sardis

Sardis, situated thirty miles south of Thyatira, was positioned between the Hermus River and Mount Tmolus. According to Pfeiffer, it was the capital of the Kingdom of Lydia, renowned for being the first to mint coins in history, a practice later adopted by the Greeks and other civilizations. The city's prosperity was fueled by its commerce, the fertile plains along the Hermus River, and the skilled production of textiles and jewelry by its artisans. During Roman times, Sardis was home to affluent followers of mystery cults, including the Cult of Cybele, which claimed the ability to revive the dead. Revelation commends a faithful few in Sardis who have kept themselves pure and are deemed worthy to walk in white with Christ (Rev 3:4).⁷⁰

Philadelphia

Philadelphia, an ancient city situated in a tributary valley of the Hermus River southeast of Sardis, was located near a volcanic zone prone to earthquakes. The city endured significant damage during the AD 17 earthquake, documented by ancient writers. Pliny the Elder described the AD 17 Lydia

---

68. Keener, *Background Commentary*, 733.

69. Brisco, *Holman Bible Atlas*, 267.

70. Keener notes that some inscriptions that were found in Asia Minor reveal that many temples prohibited worshippers with soiled garments, as their entry was seen as an insult to the deity. Pfeiffer, *Baker's Bible Atlas*, 234–35; Keener, *Background Commentary*, 735.

earthquake as the greatest earthquake in human memory.[71] Moreover, Strabo described Philadelphia as constantly shaken by earthquakes, noting that its walls remained cracked and unstable.[72] The letter to the church in Philadelphia promises, "The one who conquers, I will make him a pillar in the temple of my God," offering stability amidst a community familiar with earthquake-induced disruptions (Rev 3:12).

Laodicea

Brisco notes that Laodicea, located in the fertile Lycus Valley, was one of three cities established along a key tributary of the Meander River, which flowed westward to Miletus. Positioned between Colossae to the southeast and Hierapolis to the north, it was a major city in the affluent province of Phrygia. Renowned for its banking and textile industries, which utilized black wool from local sheep, Laodicea also gained fame for its medical school's eye salve. Revelation mentions Laodicea's wealth, encouraging believers to pursue spiritual riches and use spiritual insight similar to an eye salve, rather than relying on material wealth (3:17–18).[73]

Jerusalem

Jerusalem, Pfeiffer notes, is situated 33 miles east of the Mediterranean Sea and southeast of Joppa. It is located 14 miles west of the Dead Sea and 133 miles southwest of Damascus, with Bethlehem lying 5 miles to the south. To the east of Jerusalem, across the Kidron Valley, extends the mile-long ridge of limestone hills known as the Mount of Olives. North of the Mount of Olives, and sometimes considered a part of it, is Mount Scopus. Travelers approaching Jerusalem from the north are greeted with a sweeping view from Mount Scopus, where the Roman general Titus is said to have first glimpsed the city he was about to destroy, which he did in AD 70.[74]

---

71. Pliny the Elder, *Natural History*, 2.86.
72. Strabo, *Geography*, 13.4.10; Brisco, *Holman Bible Atlas*, 267.
73. Brisco, *Holman Bible Atlas*, 267.
74. Pfeiffer, *Baker's Bible Atlas*, 233.

LITERARY ANALYSIS

Genre

Understanding genre involves recognizing both the overall purpose of a work and the specific literary devices used within it. Dan McCartney explains that while the Gospels are primarily historical narratives, they include parables spoken by Jesus. For instance, the well-known story of the prodigal son (Luke 15:11–32), despite its historical setting, is identified as a parable due to its contextual and literary similarities with other parables, such as the parable of the sower (8:4–15).[75]

Thompson observes that if the book of Revelation were a solitary work without any comparable literature, understanding it would still necessitate a thorough examination of its text in conjunction with the historical context of its composition. Since Revelation is a work roughly contemporaneous with similar writing styles and themes, the author belongs to a tradition in which images, themes, styles, and literary forms are used to express his "psychological experiences, social perceptions, religious insights, and literary expressions."[76] In short, understanding the book of Revelation requires an appreciation of both its historical context and its genre.

Gordon D. Fee and Douglas Stuart assert that Revelation is a distinctive, intricate blend of three literary types: "apocalypse, prophecy, and letter."[77] Smalley contends that while the book should be broadly understood as prophecy, it remains challenging to precisely categorize its literary genre, noting that the traditional label of "apocalyptic" is insufficient.[78] Moreover, W. S. Vorster observes that the study of Revelation's genre is heavily influenced by the interpretive assumptions and theories of New Testament scholars as a community.[79] Given the nature of Revelation, this section will proceed on the premise that it is predominantly an apocalypse, based on

---

75. McCartney notes that a question arises: If one acknowledges variability in genre, could this be used to undermine the historical reliability of the Bible or manipulate its message? The answer lies in recognizing that a text's genre is shaped by the author's intent, which in turn is influenced by the socio-linguistic norms of their audience. McCartney and Clayton, *Let the Reader Understand*, 148–49.
76. Thompson, *Book of Revelation*, 18.
77. Fee and Stuart, *How to Read the Bible*, 259.
78. Smalley, *Revelation to John*, 7.
79. Vorster, "'Genre' and the Revelation of John," 111.

the common features it shares with other works of the same genre—a point that will be elaborated on subsequently.[80]

The term "apocalyptic" is derived from the Greek word ἀποκάλυψις (*apokalypsis*) which appears in the opening line of the book (Rev 1:1). Literarily, "apocalyptic" refers to a genre characterized by revelations about eschatological events and transcendent realities.[81] While this chapter does not aim to argue exhaustively for the apocalyptic genre classification, it will assume this framework based on observed similarities with related works. Frederick David Mazzaferri contends that arguments for Revelation's apocalyptic nature involve comparative analyses of characteristic features, though these comparisons are often either overly concise or inadequately structured.[82]

Nevertheless, it is useful to outline the general characteristics of the apocalyptic genre. Typically, this genre consists of the following four elements: (1) the writer uses a pseudonym, most often one belonging to an established tradition such as Ezra, Enoch, or Isaiah; (2) the writing is interpreted as an account of a vision, a dream, or a transcendent state; (3) the writer depicts past events as if they were in the future; and (4) there are often exhortations, prayers, and hymns.[83] Additionally, the following content is typical of the genre: (1) there are two ages—the "present age" and the "age to come"; (2) Satan is seen to control the present age, while God is portrayed as a great ruler of the age to come; (3) all people, not just Jews, are considered in the apocalypses in the sense that they are all individuals; and (4) everything is determined in advance by God, including the imminent end.[84]

To interpret Revelation accurately, it is crucial to understand both its historical context and its predominantly apocalyptic genre. James R. White points out that some people argue for a strictly literal interpretation of the

---

80. The book of Revelation incorporates elements from various genres, but it is predominantly apocalyptic. This classification is based on its shared features with other apocalyptic works, such as visions, symbolic imagery, and a focus on eschatological salvation. Scholars have categorized apocalypses into types that may or may not include an otherworldly journey by the recipient of the revelation. These types vary in their focus on historical review, cosmic or political eschatology, or personal eschatology. James C. Vanderkam, "Apocalyptic Literature," in Barton, *Cambridge Companion*, 308.

81. Vielhauer, "Introduction to Apocalypses," 582.

82. Mazzaferri, *Genre of the Book of Revelation*, 223.

83. Thompson, *Book of Revelation*, 18–19.

84. Thompson, *Book of Revelation*, 19.

Bible, rejecting the recognition of different literary forms. However, White argues, interpreting poetry literally without acknowledging its literary form misses the author's intent. Similarly, insisting on a literal reading of apocalyptic language ignores the original context and ultimately undermines the true meaning of the text.[85]

This awareness aids in recognizing the literary forms and themes used to convey its messages. Grant R. Osborne observes that readers often overlook the historical factors when interpreting apocalyptic literature like Revelation. He argues that the predictive elements tend to distract readers from the original situation, emphasizing that the author's intended meaning must take precedence.[86] Therefore, a proper grasp of these historical and literary elements is essential for a sound interpretation of Revelation.

Liturgy

The potential liturgical connections in Revelation are relevant to interpretation because they can shed light on how early Christians might have used the book in their worship. The hymns and heavenly descriptions in Revelation reflect John's focus on worship. The throne room scenes in Rev 4–5, with their vivid descriptions of heavenly worship, have led some scholars to argue for liturgical influences.[87] For instance, Paul Touilleux argued that Revelation was shaped by liturgical practices aimed at dissuading Christians from embracing cults like that of Cybele.[88]

Arthur W. Wainwright notes that while theories regarding liturgy in Revelation are largely speculative, the presence of heavenly visions and hymns in the text implies a connection to liturgical practices. Revelation 19:1–8, which features the hallelujah chorus celebrating the defeat of Babylon, could be seen as reflective of communal worship practices. It is possible that the book was intended for public reading during worship settings. However, as Wainwright notes, these interpretations, including others,

---

85. White, *Scripture Alone*, 86.
86. Osborne, *Hermeneutical Spiral*, 231.
87. Wainwright, *Mysterious Apocalypse*, 146–49.
88. Paul Touilleux explains that John employs a strategy to counter the allure of the rituals and myths associated with the "Great Mother." He aims to show the Christian faithful that these appealing elements are not only present in Christianity but are offered in a far superior form. Touilleux, *L'Apocalypse et les Cultes*, 184.

remain conjecture without conclusive proof.[89] If Revelation was influenced by or intended for liturgical settings, this could mean it was designed to reinforce communal identity, encourage perseverance through persecution, and emphasize worship of God over pagan cults.

Structure

Smalley notes that the structural analysis of the book of Revelation remains a subject of scholarly debate, with existing theories often presenting complexity and confusion. Although a narrative approach to Revelation is valid, it must be integrated with the broader "theology and interpretation of the Apocalypse."[90] Generally, there are two predominant views regarding Revelation's structure: a nonlinear, spiraling view known as recapitulation, where events are seen to repeat themselves, and a linear view, where events proceed sequentially.[91]

Recapitulation interprets the recurring cycles in Revelation as descriptions of the same eschatological situation, perceiving it from different eschatological viewpoints.[92] Aligning with the perspective of Smalley, this author argues that Revelation is structured more on theological and thematic grounds rather than chronological ones.[93] Regarding the millennium mentioned in Rev 20:1–10, this author views the thousand years as symbolic, representing an indeterminate period that corresponds to the Church Age which will be assessed in the following chapter.

Theme

Revelation 1:7 is widely regarded as the thematic verse of the book, encapsulating its central message: "Behold, he is coming with the clouds, and every eye will see him, even those who pierced him, and all tribes of the earth will wail on account of him. Even so. Amen."[94] According to Gentry, the

89. Wainwright, *Mysterious Apocalypse*, 148–49.
90. Smalley, *Revelation to John*, 19.
91. Resseguie, *Revelation of John*, 54.
92. Smalley, *Revelation to John*, 19.
93. Smalley, *Revelation to John*, 19.
94. Gentry (preterist) and Hitchcock (futurist) agree that Rev 1:7 is widely recognized as the central thematic verse of the book. Much of the information on the theme of Revelation in this section is drawn from the present author's dissertation. Gentry, *Before*

phrase "coming with the clouds" signifies Christ's judgment upon Israel, particularly in AD 70, where he uses the Roman army as the instrument of divine wrath. This interpretation aligns with the Old Testament usage of clouds as symbols of God's judgment and glory which reinforces the idea that Revelation's primary focus is on the imminent judgment of those responsible for Christ's crucifixion (cf. Pss 18:7–15; 104:3; Isa 19:1; Joel 2:1, 2; Nah 1; Zeph 1:14, 15).

Revelation 1:7 draws from at least two separate Old Testament passages, each helping to shape the understanding of John's message. In Daniel, the reference to coming "with the clouds" is not about the second coming but symbolizes the Messiah's ascension to the heavenly throne, signifying his authority over the entire earth: "And behold, with the clouds of heaven there came one like a son of man, and he came to the Ancient of Days" (Dan 7:13).[95] The text explicitly mentions that the "son of man" *ascended* to the "Ancient of Days." Thus, the passage focuses on Christ's ascension, rather than the idea of his second coming.

The reference to "those who pierced him" in Rev 1:7 clearly points to the Jewish people, as drawn from Zech 12:10, where the mourning of Israel over the Messiah is prophesied.[96] This verse highlights the judgment directed at Israel for its role in Christ's death. Gentry agrees and points out that while the Romans carried out Jesus' crucifixion, it was the Jews who instigated and demanded it (Matt 20:18–19; 27:11–25; Mark 10:33; 15:1; Luke 18:32; 23:1–2; John 18:28–31; 19:12–15; Acts 3:13; 4:26–27). He emphasizes that this view is strongly supported by the New Testament, where the apostles consistently hold the Jews accountable for Christ's crucifixion (Acts 2:22–23; 3:13–15; 5:28–30; 7:52; 10:39; 1 Thess 2:14–15).[97]

Moreover, the phrase "tribes of the earth" further supports this interpretation, as the term "tribe" (φυλή, *phylē*) is often associated with the tribes of Israel, suggesting that the judgment is specifically aimed at the Jewish nation rather than the entire world (cf. Luke 2:36; Acts 13:21; Rom 11:1; Phil 3:5; Heb 7:14).[98] Although "tribe" can also refer to gentiles when paired with broader terms in Revelation, such as "every tribe and language

---

Jerusalem Fell, 121; Hitchcock, "Domitianic Date," 80; Quintern, "Neronic Date," 76–82.

95. Wilson, *Commentary*, 7; Rogers, *Prophecy of Daniel*, 24.

96. Wilson, *Commentary*, 7.

97. Gentry, *Navigating*, 94. See also Ratton, *Apocalypse of St. John*, 129; Stuart, *Commentary on the Apocalypse*, 1:272–73; Terry, *Apocalypse of John*, 33.

98. Gentry, *Beast of Revelation*, 119–20.

and people and nation" (cf. Rev 5:9), this expansion does not apply to Rev 1:7, indicating that "the tribes" in this context specifically pertains to the Jews.[99] Therefore, the most accurate interpretation appears to be that "the tribes" in this verse specifically refers to the Jewish people. The theme of Revelation centers on the judgment of Israel in the first century, with Christ's coming "with the clouds" symbolizing the divine retribution upon the apostate Jews responsible for his crucifixion.

SUMMARY

Chapter 6 lays a foundational understanding of Revelation by exploring its historical, cultural, geographical, and literary contexts. It highlights arguments for an early date during Nero's reign, situating the book in the first century through references like Nero as the sixth king and the cryptic number 666. The cultural backdrop includes the Herodian dynasty's relationship with Rome, the imperial cult's influence, and Judea's economic conditions, revealing the sociopolitical pressures on early Christians. Geographically, Patmos and the seven churches of Rev 2–3 provide insights into challenges faced by these communities which strengthens one's understanding of the text's prophetic messages.

The literary context emphasizes Revelation as an apocalyptic work, drawing on genre conventions such as symbolic imagery and eschatological themes. Recognizing its apocalyptic nature allows for an appropriate interpretive approach that respects both its literary style and historical context. The book's structure, incorporating elements of letters, hymns, and visions, highlights its dual role as both a theological treatise and a practical guide for first-century Christian communities. Finally, the theme of Revelation is shown to be one of divine judgment directed at the Jewish people for their role in the crucifixion of Christ.

---

99. Gentry, *Before Jerusalem Fell*, 127–28; Quintern, "Neronic Date," 79–80.

Chapter Seven

Interpreting Revelation

EXPOSITION OF KEY PASSAGES

In this chapter, an exegesis of key passages from the book of Revelation using the grammatical-historical method of interpretation and the partial-preterist approach will be provided. As mentioned, this method involves examining the historical context, literary context, consulting the original languages for meaning, and exploring the sources of John's imagery. By employing this method, one can gain a clearer understanding of the text and discern the original meaning intended for John's initial audience.

Revelation 1:1–9

> The revelation of Jesus Christ, which God gave him to show to his servants the things that must soon take place. He made it known by sending his angel to his servant John, who bore witness to the word of God and to the testimony of Jesus Christ, even to all that he saw. Blessed is the one who reads aloud the words of this prophecy, and blessed are those who hear, and who keep what is written in it, for the time is near. John to the seven churches that are in Asia: Grace to you and peace from him who is and who was and who is to come, and from the seven spirits who are before his throne, and from Jesus Christ the faithful witness, the firstborn of the dead, and the ruler of kings on earth. To him who loves us and has freed us from our sins by his blood and made us a kingdom, priests to his God and Father, to him be glory and dominion forever and ever. Amen. Behold, he is coming with the clouds, and every eye will see him, even those who pierced him, and all tribes

of the earth will wail on account of him. Even so. Amen. "I am the Alpha and the Omega," says the Lord God, "who is and who was and who is to come, the Almighty." I, John, your brother and partner in the tribulation and the kingdom and the patient endurance that are in Jesus, was on the island called Patmos on account of the word of God and the testimony of Jesus. (Rev 1:1–9)

Revelation 1:1–9 serves as the prologue to the book of Revelation, introducing its divine source, intended recipients, and the immediate relevance of its prophecies. This passage emphasizes that the revelation is of Jesus Christ, conveyed to his servant John through symbolic language that discloses truths. A thorough examination of the Greek text and historical context reveals that John's message was directed towards first-century Christians facing persecution, with an expectation of imminent fulfillment.

The opening verses of Revelation introduce the work as a revelation (ἀποκάλυψις, *apokalypsis*) of Jesus Christ, meant to unveil and make manifest divine truths (Rev 1:1). The term "revelation" itself is significant, indicating an unveiling or disclosure of what was previously hidden.[1] The verb "made it known" (ἐσήμανεν, *esēmanen*) from the verb σημαίνω, *sēmainō*, characteristically Johannine, implies more than mere indication; it signifies disclosing deep, often symbolic, realities (cf. John 12:33; 18:32).[2] This prepares one to understand Revelation as a symbolic and metaphorical text, warning against purely literal interpretations.

Three times in the prologue (Rev 1:1–5) the full designation, "Jesus Chris," is used, highlighting the divine authority and significance of the message being conveyed. The prophecy is presented as pertaining to events whose time is near, with the terms "shortly" (ἐν τάχει, *en tachei*) and "near" (ἐγγύς, *eggus*) emphasizing temporal immediacy (Rev 1:1, 3; 22:6, 10).[3] These terms clearly convey John's expectation that the prophecies would be fulfilled shortly after their writing.

John's use of terms indicating temporal nearness is deliberate, stressing that the prophecies were to occur imminently. Critics, such as Mounce,

---

1. Smalley, *Revelation to John*, 27.

2. Robert Mounce, in his commentary on Revelation, highlights the importance of the symbolic nature of the text. He notes that the term σημαίνω carries the connotation of signifying or making known through signs. Mounce points out that this method of communication is intended to convey deeper spiritual truths through symbolic language, thus requiring careful interpretation to uncover the intended meanings. Mounce, *Revelation*, 42.

3. Gentry, *Book of Revelation*, 19. See also Danker et al., *Lexicon*, 992–93.

suggest that "soon" does not necessarily imply immediacy, citing Paul's reference to God "soon" crushing Satan in Rom 16:20.[4] However, in Romans, Paul is addressing a specific situation within the Roman church, dealing with divisions and false teachings. The "crushing of Satan" should be interpreted as God's intervention to resolve these specific issues. Mounce's interpretation ignores the specific context of Revelation as apocalyptic literature, which emphasizes urgency regarding divine intervention.

Mounce argues that the expression "must soon take place" should be read with the understanding that the end is always imminent and that "chronological sequence is of secondary concern."[5] Nevertheless, this perspective should also be seen as overlooking the immediate pastoral and prophetic intent of John's message to his original audience. The repeated use of terms like "soon" and "near" throughout the book (1:1, 3; 2:16; 3:11; 11:14; 22:6, 7, 10, 12, 20) supports the expectation of immediate fulfillment from the perspective of the original audience.[6]

Revelation was written to first-century Christians facing persecution, a fact evident from John's own exile (Rev 1:9). The early date for the book's composition, during Nero's reign, aligns with the intense persecution Christians faced starting in AD 64. Nero's systematic persecution, as opposed to the lack of evidence for such under Domitian, supports the early dating of Revelation and its immediate relevance to the original audience (see chapter 6).[7]

The letter is addressed to specific church communities in Asia Minor, as seen in the letters to the seven churches (Rev 1:10–11). The order of these cities follows a Roman courier route, indicating practical communication methods and the intention to address real historical churches facing contemporary issues.[8] This specificity further highlights that John's prophecies were not distant predictions but addressed immediate challenges for first-century Christians.

Revelation 1:7 serves as the thematic verse, depicting Christ's coming in judgment upon Israel, specifically in AD 70. The phrase "coming

---

4. Mounce, *Revelation*, 41.

5. Mounce, *Revelation*, 41.

6. For more information about the temporal expectation of the author, see Gentry, *Before Jerusalem Fell*, 133–45; Quintern, "Neronic Date," 85–87.

7. Even proponents of a late date for the book of Revelation acknowledge that there is insufficient evidence to substantiate the notion of systematic persecution of Christians during Domitian's reign. Boring, *Revelation*, 17.

8. Ramsay, *Letters to the Seven*, 186.

with the clouds" symbolizes divine judgment (cf. Pss 18:7–15; 104:3; Isa 19:1; Joel 2:1–2; Nah 1; Zeph 1:14–15).[9] This is consistent with Old and New Testament references to divine judgment and Christ's return in clouds (Matt 24:3; 26:64; Acts 1:11; 1 Thess 4:15–17).[10] The reference to "those who pierced him" (Rev 1:7), drawn from Zech 12:10, clearly refers to the Jewish people, reinforcing the idea of judgment upon them for instigating Christ's crucifixion (Matt 20:18–19; 27:11–25; Mark 10:33; 15:1; Luke 18:32; 23:1–2; John 18:28–31; 19:12–15; Acts 3:13; 4:26–27).[11]

Revelation 1:1–9, examined through the grammatical-historical method, reveals that John's prophecies were directed towards first-century Christians facing imminent persecution, with the expectation of immediate fulfillment. The symbolic language, historical context, and specific addressing of contemporary churches all point to the relevance of these prophecies to John's original audience. The thematic verse highlights the judgment upon Israel, further reinforcing the immediate applicability of Revelation to the first-century context.

Revelation 11:1–2

> Then I was given a measuring rod like a staff, and I was told, "Rise and measure the temple of God and the altar and those who worship there, but do not measure the court outside the temple; leave that out, for it is given over to the nations, and they will trample the holy city for forty-two months. (Rev 11:1–2)

This passage is rich with symbolic actions and implications. To provide a thorough exegesis, this section will, again, focus on the grammatical and historical context, emphasizing the original language and relevant Old Testament scriptures. First, the term "measuring rod" (κάλαμος, *kalamos*) refers to a reed or measuring tool often used in symbolic contexts in prophetic literature (cf. Ezek 40:3).[12] The act of measuring (μέτρησον, *metreson*) signifies an act of delineation or separation. The objects to be measured include the temple of God (likely the holy of holies), the altar (referring

---

9. Gentry, *Before Jerusalem Fell*, 123.
10. Gentry, *Before Jerusalem Fell*, 123.
11. Gentry, *Navigating*, 94. For more information regarding the thematic focus of Revelation, see Gentry, *Before Jerusalem Fell*, 121–32; Quintern, "Neronic Date," 76–83.
12. Morris, *Revelation of St. John*, 145.

to the altar of incense within the temple, cf. Heb 9:4), and the worshipers, indicating the faithful believers.

In verse 2, John is instructed *not* to measure the court outside the temple, referred to as the "Court of the Gentiles," a distinct part of the Second Temple where gentiles were permitted (cf. 1 Kgs 8:41–43; 2 Chr 4:9; Isa 56:7; Ezek 40:17).[13] The verb "leave that out" or "cast out" (ἔκβαλε, *ekbale*) suggests a forceful exclusion, indicating its defilement and rejection. Gentry observes that this term can signify exorcism, excommunication, or divorce, emphasizing a significant separation between the holy and the profane.[14] The outer court, left unmeasured and given over to the nations (ἔθνεσιν, *ethnēsin*), symbolizes judgment upon the apostate Jews and desecration by the gentiles.

The period during which the gentiles will trample the holy city is described as forty-two months, corresponding to three and a half years. This time frame recurs throughout Revelation, signifying a period of intense tribulation (cf. Rev 11:2, 3; 12:6, 14; 13:5).[15] The trampling of the holy city (Jerusalem) for forty-two months aligns historically with Nero's persecution of Christians from November AD 64 until his suicide in June AD 68 and the Jewish-Roman War, which culminated in the destruction of the Second Temple in AD 70. Luke 21:24, which describes Jerusalem being overrun by gentiles, parallels this passage, depicting a period of desolation and judgment.

Therefore, this study concludes that Rev 11:1–2 reveals a divine act of measuring that symbolizes protection for the faithful while marking the apostate for judgment. The forceful expulsion of the outer court, given over to the gentiles, aligns with historical events of the first century, notably Nero's persecution and the Jewish-Roman War. The period of forty-two months serves as both a symbolic and literal time frame of tribulation which highlights the fulfillment of prophetic judgment upon Jerusalem.

Revelation 13:1–4

> And I saw a beast rising out of the sea, with ten horns and seven heads, with ten diadems on its horns and blasphemous names on

---

13. Wilson, *Commentary*, 126.
14. Gentry, *Divorce of Israel*, 2:910–19.
15. Terry, *Apocalypse of John*, 133–34; Wilson, *Commentary*, 127.

its heads. And the beast that I saw was like a leopard; its feet were like a bear's, and its mouth was like a lion's mouth. And to it the dragon gave his power and his throne and great authority. One of its heads seemed to have a mortal wound, but its mortal wound was healed, and the whole earth marveled as they followed the beast. And they worshiped the dragon, for he had given his authority to the beast, and they worshiped the beast, saying, "Who is like the beast, and who can fight against it?" (Rev 13:1–4)

The symbolism of the beast in Rev 13:1–4 draws heavily from the vision of the four beasts in Dan 7, where each beast represents a successive world empire. In Daniel's vision, the beasts emerge from the sea, signifying raging gentile nations (Dan 7:2–3). The four beasts in Daniel are distinct, representing Babylon, Medo-Persia, Greece, and Rome, respectively.[16] However, in John's vision, the two beasts are contemporaneous, with the second beast serving as a satellite of the first, exercising its authority (Rev 13:12).[17] This distinction highlights John's independent adaptation of Daniel's symbols to construct a unique apocalyptic picture relevant to his context.

Revelation 13:1 depicts a beast rising from the sea with ten horns and seven heads, each with a blasphemous name. Gentry notes that the sea here likely has a dual significance. Geographically, from the perspective of Israel or Asia Minor, Rome would appear to rise out of the Mediterranean Sea.[18] Roman troops historically invaded the eastern Mediterranean from the sea, linking the beast's emergence to the contemporary political situation. Symbolically, the sea represents gentile nations, as seen in various Old Testament passages (Ps 2:1; Isa 17:12; 57:20; 60:5; Jer 6:22–23; 51:42; Ezek 26:3).[19] Thus, the beast rising from the sea likely alludes to the Roman Empire.

Smalley emphasizes the significance of Rome's seven hills in understanding the symbolism. Rome, famously known as the "city of seven hills," provides a geographical and symbolic reference that would have been evident to contemporary readers (see chapter 6).[20] This association between the seven heads and Roman emperors highlights the dual nature of the beast as both a kingdom and its rulers. Even Mounce states, "There is little

---

16. Storms, *Kingdom Come*, 95.
17. Terry, *Apocalypse of John*, 169.
18. Gentry, *Divorce of Israel*, 2:1047–48.
19. Gentry, *Divorce of Israel*, 2:1048.
20. Smalley, *Revelation to John*, 435.

doubt that for John the beast was the Roman Empire as persecutor of the church."[21]

Revelation 13:3 presents one of the heads as having a mortal wound that was healed. Mathison notes that this imagery is complex and open to interpretation. He discusses the difficulty of translating the Greek word *mian* (μίαν), which can be rendered as either a cardinal number ("one") or an ordinal number ("the first").[22] If translated as a cardinal number, the verse may refer to the survival of the Roman Empire following Nero's death. If translated as an ordinal number, it may refer to the Roman Empire's survival after Julius Caesar's assassination in 44 BC.[23] David Aune, as noted by Mathison, suggests that the pronoun *autou* (αὐτοῦ) in the phrase refers to the beast rather than the head, indicating that while one head is mortally wounded, it is the beast (the Roman Empire) that recovers, symbolizing the empire's resilience and continuity despite internal turmoil.[24]

John's depiction of the beast allows for flexibility in its symbolic language. The beast with seven heads represents both a kingdom and individual rulers. Revelation 17:9–10 describes this symbolism, explaining that the seven heads are seven kings, five of whom have fallen, one who is, and one who is yet to come. This interpretation suggests a succession of Roman emperors, with the beast representing the collective Roman Empire and individual emperors, as argued in chapter 6 of this present work.

THE BABYLONIAN HARLOT

Revelation 17:1–6

> Then one of the seven angels who had the seven bowls came and said to me, "Come, I will show you the judgment of the great prostitute who is seated on many waters, with whom the kings of the earth have committed sexual immorality, and with the wine of whose sexual immorality the dwellers on earth have become drunk." And he carried me away in the Spirit into a wilderness, and I saw a woman sitting on a scarlet beast that was full of blasphemous names, and it had seven heads and ten horns. The

---

21. Mounce, *Revelation*, 246.
22. Mathison, *From Age to Age*, 678.
23. Mathison, *From Age to Age*, 678.
24. Mathison, *From Age to Age*, 678. See also Aune, *Revelation 6–16*, 736.

woman was arrayed in purple and scarlet, and adorned with gold and jewels and pearls, holding in her hand a golden cup full of abominations and the impurities of her sexual immorality. And on her forehead was written a name of mystery: "Babylon the great, mother of prostitutes and of earth's abominations." And I saw the woman, drunk with the blood of the saints, the blood of the martyrs of Jesus. (Rev 17:1–6)

Revelation 17:1–6 describes the vision of the great harlot, a symbolic figure that has sparked extensive theological debate. This passage, along with others in Revelation, has led to various interpretations regarding Babylon and the harlot's identity and significance. For instance, Giancarlo Biguzzi identifies five traditional interpretations of Babylon: (1) the historical city on the Euphrates, (2) the "city of the devil" manifesting in every era, (3) the eschatological city of the antichrist, (4) Imperial Rome, and (5) Jerusalem.[25]

While Biguzzi supports the Roman identification, this present author argues that both Babylon and the harlot in Revelation refer to Jerusalem, as further detailed in the author's article critiquing Biguzzi's position.[26] To support this identification, this section will present five key arguments, supported by scriptural, historical, and theological evidence: collaboration with Roman authorities, economic prosperity under Roman rule, symbolic attire of the harlot, identification of the "Great City," and historical persecution of prophets and Christians. The grammatical-historical method will continue to be used to interpret the book of Revelation in its original context, providing a solid foundation for this interpretation.

The image of the Babylonian harlot riding the beast (Rev 17:3) symbolizes Jerusalem's collaboration with Roman authorities during the first century.[27] Jewish leadership, especially the Sadducees and the high priestly class, maintained their dominance by aligning with Rome. The Sadducees, primarily composed of wealthy priests and aristocrats, balanced traditional religious doctrines with practical political strategies, cooperating with Rome to protect their authority.[28] This compromised alliance is evident in

---

25. Biguzzi, "Babylon," 372.

26. The following arguments in this section are drawn extensively from this author's forthcoming article, Quintern, "Babylon Unveiled."

27. Gentry, *He Shall Have Dominion*, 387.

28. Ferguson, *Backgrounds*, 519–20.

the trial and crucifixion of Jesus, where Jewish leaders sought Roman consent for execution (Matt 27:11-26).

Economically, Jerusalem thrived under Roman rule, benefiting from the stability and infrastructure provided by the *Pax Romana*.[29] Herod's reign brought substantial prosperity and massive construction projects, including the reconstruction of the Second Temple, facilitated by his close relationship with Rome.[30] This collaboration led to economic growth and increased Jerusalem's religious significance which demonstrated the benefits of Herod's alignment with Roman authorities.

The harlot's attire in Rev 17:4-5—gold, scarlet, and purple—parallels the description of the high priest's robes in Josephus's writings.[31] Furthermore, the Second Temple's golden gate and Babylonian-style curtain, embroidered with blue, fine linen, scarlet, and purple, strengthen this association.[32] These color connections imply that the harlot represents Jerusalem, reflecting both the sacred garments of the high priest and the architectural elements of the Second Temple.

The harlot in Revelation is identified as "Babylon the great" (17:5) and is repeatedly referred to as "the great city" (16:19; 17:18; 18:10-21). The phrase "the great city" first appears in Rev 11:8, where it refers to the location where their "Lord was crucified," unmistakably pointing to Jerusalem. Gentry argues that, according to the principle of first mention, the initial use of a descriptor establishes its meaning for subsequent uses.[33] Thus, the consistent reference to "the great city" throughout Revelation reinforces the identification of the harlot with Jerusalem, the city where Jesus was crucified (Matt 23:34-37).

---

29. The *Pax Romana* denotes a two hundred-year era of peace in the Roman Empire, spanning from 27 BC to AD 180, characterized by minimal warfare and significant cultural and economic development. Levine, *Judaism and Hellenism*, 46; Rosenstein, *Turning Points in Jewish History*, 113; Quintern, "Babylon Unveiled."

30. As a client king, Herod skillfully incorporated his kingdom into the Roman Empire, demonstrating his political allegiance through various alliances with Rome. This integration is evident in different aspects of his reign. For example, his court included many non-Jewish members with Greek or Latin names, and his coins featured Greek inscriptions and Roman symbols. Levine, *Judaism and Hellenism*, 48. See also Ferguson, *Backgrounds*, 413-17.

31. Gentry observes that the apostle John (Rev 17:4-5) places significant emphasis on the Babylonian harlot's attire, vividly detailing her lavish adornments. Gentry, *Navigating*, 151; Josephus, *Jewish War*, 5.5.7. Quintern, "Babylon Unveiled."

32. Gentry, *Navigating*, 153; Josephus, *Jewish War*, 5.5.4.

33. Gentry, *Book of Revelation*, 75.

Revelation 17:6 depicts the harlot as being "drunk with the blood of the saints." This imagery aligns with Jerusalem's historical role in persecuting prophets and early Christians, as documented in the Gospels and Acts. Both Jesus and Stephen condemned Jerusalem for its violent opposition to God's messengers.[34] Stephen, the first Christian martyr, accused the Jewish leaders in Jerusalem of betraying and murdering the "Righteous One" and persecuting the prophets who foretold his coming (Acts 7:52). This persistent theme of persecution supports the view that Jerusalem is the harlot, symbolizing spiritual adultery and hostility toward God's work through Christ and his followers.

The term "harlot" is a well-established designation for Jerusalem within the prophetic tradition of the Old Testament, symbolizing Israel's unfaithfulness to God. Prophets like Hosea, Ezekiel, Isaiah, and Jeremiah used this metaphor to depict Jerusalem as an unfaithful wife breaking her covenant with the Lord through idolatry and illicit foreign alliances. For instance, in Ezek 16, Jerusalem is depicted as an unfaithful wife who breaks her covenant with God by engaging in idolatry with foreign nations. Similarly, in Hosea, the prophet is commanded to marry a promiscuous woman to symbolize Israel's infidelity: "take to yourself a wife of whoredome" (Hos 1:2). Additional references include Isa 1:21; Jer 2:2, 20; 3:1, 2, 6, 8; 4:30; 11:15; and 13:27. This metaphor could not apply to Rome or other gentile cities, as they did not share a covenant relationship with God.[35]

John's use of harlotry imagery in Revelation to describe Jerusalem highlights the city's spiritual adultery, particularly its rejection of Jesus Christ, the Messiah (Matt 12:14; 26:3–4, 59; 27:1). This rejection is epitomized by the crucifixion of Christ in "the great city," called the harlot (Rev 17:4–5; cf. 11:8; 16:19; 17:18; 18:10–21). Jerusalem, as the political and religious center of Judaism and a symbol of national and religious identity, would have been deeply resonant with John's audience, communicating the gravity of the city's spiritual apostasy.[36]

---

34. Jesus laments over Jerusalem (Matt 23:37), saying, "O Jerusalem, Jerusalem, the city that kills the prophets and stones those who are sent to it!" Beagley, *"Sitz im Leben,"* 94; cf. Biguzzi, "Babylon," 377; Quintern, "Babylon Unveiled."

35. For more information, see Russell, *Parousia*, 482–97; Gregg, *Revelation*, 460–68; Ford, *Revelation*, 285; Gentry, *He Shall Have Dominion*, 384–88.

36. For example, Tacitus discussed the siege and destruction of Jerusalem, highlighting its significance to the Jewish people. Tacitus, *Histories*, 5.8–5.12. See also Quintern, "Babylon Unveiled."

Interpreting Revelation

EXPOSITION OF THE MILLENNIUM

Revelation 20:1–3

> Then I saw an angel coming down from heaven, holding in his hand the key to the bottomless pit and a great chain. And he seized the dragon, that ancient serpent, who is the devil and Satan, and bound him for a thousand years, and threw him into the pit, and shut it and sealed it over him, so that he might not deceive the nations any longer, until the thousand years were ended. After that he must be released for a little while. (Rev 20:1–3)

The term "millennium" comes from the Latin words *mille*, meaning "one thousand," and *annum*, meaning "year," thus referring to a period of "one thousand years." In biblical contexts, "thousand" often symbolizes a large, indefinite number, indicating vastness or completeness rather than a precise measurement (see Mic 6:7; Rev 5:11).[37] For example, God's ownership of "the cattle on a thousand hills" (Ps 50:10) signifies his dominion over all creation, not a literal count of hills.

Boettner explains that the book of Revelation is filled with figurative and symbolic language. For instance, the seven golden candlesticks represent the churches of Asia, and the seven spirits before the throne symbolize the fullness of the Holy Spirit.[38] The number twelve is significant as it symbolizes the church, seen in the twelve apostles, the twenty-four elders, or the 144,000, representing God's elect. Boettner also points out that the number ten in the Bible signifies completeness, as seen in the Ten Commandments, the ten plagues of Egypt, and the dimensions of the holy of holies.[39] A thousand, being the cube of ten, symbolizes vastness in number or time. In Rev 20, Boettner rightly argues that imagery, such as the dragon, serpent, and the thousand-year reign, should be understood symbolically, not literally. He notes that Calvin likewise interpreted the "thousand years" metaphorically, dismissing a literal interpretation as a simplistic and unworthy notion.[40]

---

37. David Chilton explains that "one thousand" in the Bible often denotes fullness or completeness, similar to how the number seven symbolizes quality. Chilton, *Days of Vengeance*, 506. See also Dockery, *Commentary*, 678; Storms, *Kingdom Come*, 456.

38. Boettner, *Millennium*, 63.

39. Boettner, *Millennium*, 63.

40. Calvin, *Institutes*, 3.25.5; Boettner, *Millennium*, 64–65.

In verse 1, the phrase "Then I saw" denotes the order in which John was given the vision rather than a strict chronology of events. Fee and Stuart note that apocalyptic literature often employs symbolic numbers, presenting visions in carefully organized sets that convey a thematic message without insisting on strict chronological order.[41] Thus, interpreting these events sequentially may be misleading.

For instance, if one interprets Rev 20:1–3 chronologically, it raises a contradiction with the preceding events in 19:19–21. In 20:1–3, a procedure is described to prevent Satanic deception of nations previously deceived in 19:19–21. This seems inconsistent since defending nations from Satan's deception after they have already been deceived by Satan and eliminated by Christ (19:12–21) appears illogical.[42] The narrative of Satan's conquest in 20:1–3 seems to have parallels in 12:7–9, where the same names (dragon, serpent, devil, Satan) are mentioned, perhaps reinforcing the non-linear nature of the narrative.[43]

Gentry, however, suggests a nuanced interpretation concerning the relationship between Rev 20:1–3 and the preceding vision outlined in Rev 12:7–17.[44] The depiction in Rev 12 illustrates Satan's expulsion from heaven to earth, accompanied by his angels, culminating in an intensified persecution of the saints for a brief duration. In contrast, 20:1–3 portrays Satan's solitary casting into the abyss from the earth, where he is subsequently restrained from inflicting harm upon the saints for an extended period. This differentiation is significant as it explains the consequences of Satan's expulsion as detailed in 12:7–17 and following. In this passage, Satan's role extends to empowering the "sea beast" and subsequently utilizing the "land beast" as its subordinate. The sea beast is depicted as engaging in deceitful activities (13:14; 19:20), in conjunction with the harlot (18:23), actions which 20:3 seems to preclude through Satan's binding.[45]

At any rate, this verse does not suggest a literal binding of the devil with physical chains, as Satan is a spiritual being (cf. John 8:44; Eph 6:12; 2 Cor 10:3–4; 1 Pet 5:8). Specific language is being used to highlight that the devil is bound in terms of deceiving the nations (πλανήσῃ, *planēsēi*).[46]

---

41. Fee and Stuart, *How to Read the Bible*, 261.
42. Storms, *Kingdom Come*, 431.
43. Aune, *Revelation 17–22*, 1078.
44. Gentry, *Divorce of Israel*, 2:1545.
45. Gentry, *Divorce of Israel*, 2:1545.
46. The Greek verb πλανήσῃ carries the meaning of "leading astray" or "deceiving."

John draws on early Jewish texts, such as 1 En 10:4–6; 88:1, which speak of wicked angels being chained until the day of Judgment.[47] Here, John employs this imagery to convey that the devil cannot hinder the spread of the gospel among the nations. The phrase "he must be released for a little while" indicates that after an unspecified duration (symbolized by the thousand years), Satan is briefly set free to lead a rebellion before facing ultimate destruction (cf. Rev 20:10).

Revelation 20:4–6

> Then I saw thrones, and seated on them were those to whom the authority to judge was committed. Also I saw the souls of those who had been beheaded for the testimony of Jesus and for the word of God, and those who had not worshiped the beast or its image and had not received its mark on their foreheads or their hands. They came to life and reigned with Christ for a thousand years. The rest of the dead did not come to life until the thousand years were ended. This is the first resurrection. Blessed and holy is the one who shares in the first resurrection! Over such the second death has no power, but they will be priests of God and of Christ, and they will reign with him for a thousand years. (Rev 20:4–6)

In this verse, the "thrones" in heaven correspond to those occupied by the twenty-four elders mentioned in Rev 4:4, symbolizing the church or the elect.[48] This parallels the description of souls beheaded and those slain at the fifth seal's breaking in 6:9.[49] Christ, as king, establishes an order where he shares authority with the martyrs. The thousand-year period refers to the same thousand-year period above, i.e., the Church Age.

The "first resurrection" pertains to Jesus Christ's resurrection, and only those in Christ share in it. The second resurrection, occurring at the end of the Church Age, involves a general resurrection and judgment. Christ, identified as the "firstfruits" and "firstborn from the dead," signifies

---

In the New Testament, it portrays the action of guiding someone away from the truth, usually associated with moral or spiritual deception (cf. Matt 24:24; 1 John 2:26). Danker et al., *Lexicon*, 822. See also Wilson, *Commentary*, 230.

47. For example, 1 En 10:4–6 depicts God commanding the archangel Raphael to bind the fallen angel Azazel, casting him into darkness and covering him with rough rocks until the day of judgment. See also Keener, *Background Commentary*, 770.

48. Mathison, *Postmillennialism*, 156.

49. Paul, *Revelation*, 328.

the foundational resurrection (1 Cor 15:20; Col 1:18).[50] Gentry suggests that John contrasts the martyrs in Rev 20:4 with the enemies killed in the AD 70 judgment (19:19–21). He notes that John encourages the believers to endure martyrdom if required (1:9; 2:9, 26; 3:9–10, 21), assuring them that God will judge their aggressors, reward and resurrect the believers in heaven, while their enemies remain awaiting judgment (20:4–5, 11–15).[51] Through faith, believers partake in Jesus' death and resurrection (Rom 6:4–5), ensuring immunity from the second death for those in the first resurrection. In contrast, the second resurrection leads to an "agonizing realization of eternity" for those facing the second death.[52]

Revelation 20:7–10

> And when the thousand years are ended, Satan will be released from his prison and will come out to deceive the nations that are at the four corners of the earth, Gog and Magog, to gather them for battle; their number is like the sand of the sea. And they marched up over the broad plain of the earth and surrounded the camp of the saints and the beloved city, but fire came down from heaven and consumed them, and the devil who had deceived them was thrown into the lake of fire and sulfur where the beast and the false prophet were, and they will be tormented day and night forever and ever. (Rev 20:7–8)

At the end of the Church Age, Satan will be unleashed for a final rebellion against the kingdom of God. This allusion is rooted in the symbolic adversaries "Gog and Magog" from Ezek 38 and 39, often regarded in Jewish texts as the "final major enemies of Israel."[53] God will allow Satan to raise a wicked army who will eventually be cast into the lake of fire. In response to Satan's deception of nations and the instigation of rebellion, God intervenes by sending fire from heaven to annihilate his enemies (Rev 20:9). This likely refers to the second coming of Christ, "In flaming fire, inflicting vengeance on those who do not know God and on those who do not obey the gospel

---

50. Wilson, *Commentary*, 233.
51. Gentry, *Divorce of Israel*, 2:1586.
52. Patterson, *Revelation*, 294–95.
53. Keener, *Background Commentary*, 771.

of our Lord Jesus" (2 Thess 1:8).⁵⁴ Ultimately, the narrative concludes with Satan and his followers being cast into hell for eternity (Rev 20:10).

Additionally, Gentry observes that John uses the indefinite future clause of time (ὅταν τελεσθῇ, *hotan telesthē*), which can be translated as "whenever," implying that the "thousand years" are not meant to be taken literally. He argues that if it were a literal thousand years, John would not say "whenever the thousand years are finished," since the exact time would be known. However, it still signifies a historical period of some duration because those years will ultimately be completed (τελεσθῇ), leading to Satan's binding until that time.⁵⁵

Hitchcock brings forth a question regarding the specific nature of Satan's final release (Rev 20:7–9). He posits that the partial-preterist position is incorrect because the final release of Satan did not happen "soon" after Revelation was written. The answer to this question lies in the preceding verses, where it is stated that Satan is initially bound, preventing him from deceiving the nations (Rev 20:3; cf. Matt 12:29). However, as time unfolds, there comes a moment when Satan is once again allowed to lead nations astray. This has not yet taken place, as it occurs *after* the successful evangelization of the world. From the perspective of postmillennialism, the "thousand years" signifies an extensive time frame during which the Great Commission is fulfilled (Matt 28:18–20). Following this period, God permits Satan to resume his deception, but ultimately, the Lord returns and sentences the wicked to eternal damnation (2 Thess 1:8).⁵⁶

APPLICATION

The chief concern of John in Revelation is not the timing of the second coming but the assurance that Christ's followers, who endure present sufferings, will be vindicated by his return, as noted by David S. Dockery, a premillennialist.⁵⁷ This hope should influence current actions, urging for

---

54. Gentry agrees, "This fire from heaven appears to picture Christ's second advent at the end of history, for it is followed by the final judgment ([Rev] 20:11ff.)." Gentry, *Divorce of Israel*, 2:1600.

55. Gentry, *Divorce of Israel*, 2:1589.

56. Hitchcock, "Domitianic Date," 89–90; Gentry, *Postmillennialism*, 5–8. See also Terry, *Apocalypse of John*, 242–43; Wilson, *Commentary*, 236; Mathison, *Postmillennialism*, 156–57; Bahnsen, *Victory in Jesus*, 40–42.

57. Dockery, *Commentary*, 679.

perseverance in anticipation of God's victory (Rom 8:18–25). Additionally, Rev 20:1–10 shapes one's eschatological views, impacting interpretations throughout Scripture and evangelization efforts.[58] For instance, Sandlin emphasizes that eschatological beliefs drive different practices: those expecting imminent doom may neglect evangelization, while those anticipating a Christianized world before Christ's return will have different priorities and expectations.[59] Thus, the way believers interpret Revelation influences their present conduct and mission, shaping their engagement with the world in light of their eschatological hopes and convictions.

SUMMARY

This chapter has provided a brief exposition of key passages in the book of Revelation using a partial-preterist lens and the grammatical-historical method of interpretation. The exploration of these passages has not only clarified their symbolic nuances but has anchored them firmly in their first-century context, highlighting the immediate relevance and urgency of John's messages to his contemporaries. This approach reaffirms that the events described were expected to unfold swiftly, providing both hope and warning to the early Christian communities under persecution.

---

58. On this, Grenz writes, "In this sense [postmillennialism] forms a positive counterbalance to the tendency towards disengagement that often characterizes premillennialism. It is no historical accident that by and large the great thrusts toward worldwide evangelistic outreach and social concern in the modern era were launched by a church imbued with the optimism that characterizes postmillennial thinking." Grenz, *Millennial Maze*, 185. See also Davis, *Christ's Victorious Kingdom*, 119.

59. Sandlin, *Postmillennial Primer*, xxvi.

Chapter Eight

Response to Common Objections

THEOLOGICAL OBJECTIONS

This chapter explores several objections commonly raised against postmillennialism. While this discussion cannot exhaustively address every objection, it aims to engage with key critiques, drawing primarily from the insights of Gentry, along with considerations from Mathison, and others. While acknowledging that challenges to postmillennialism are varied and multifaceted, this chapter will simply focus on engaging with several of the most prevalent objections.[1]

Human Depravity and Sin

The argument against postmillennialism, based on the biblical doctrine of sin, asserts that the inherent sinfulness of humanity renders it impossible for the church to bring about the successful completion of the Great Commission.[2] This perspective suggests that the pervasive nature of sin precludes the reality or plausibility of postmillennialism. However, a thorough

---

1. For a comprehensive examination of objections to postmillennialism, see Gentry, *He Shall Have Dominion*, 427–515. Conversely, for an extensive critique of the postmillennial position, consult LaHaye and Ice, *End Times Controversy*.

2. Bahnsen notes that postmillennialism has frequently been subject to misinterpretation and misrepresentation, occasionally being depicted as espousing a belief in humanity's intrinsic goodness or as lacking resilience against the progression towards liberal ideologies. For example, see Walvoord, *Millennial Kingdom*, 34–35; Lindsey and Carlson, *Late Great Planet Earth*, 164; Bahnsen, *Victory in Jesus*, 75.

examination of postmillennial theology demonstrates that this objection misunderstands the nature of salvation.

For instance, Gentry addresses this objection by highlighting a fundamental aspect of the Christian faith: the transformative power of the gospel. He argues that dismissing postmillennialism on the grounds of sin inadvertently discounts the reality of salvation itself. Despite the pervasive presence of sin, countless sinners have converted to Christ throughout history. Each convert was once a totally depraved, unregenerate sinner, yet they experienced the saving power of the gospel, which is "the power of God unto salvation" (Rom 1:16). The same power that saves one sinner can save many, demonstrating that the presence of sin does not negate the possibility of widespread gospel success.[3]

Mathison presents four key reasons supporting this position. First, it is no more challenging for God to sovereignly save many sinners than it is for him to save one sinner. The doctrine of total depravity acknowledges that every sinner is equally in need of divine grace, and God's sovereign power is fully capable of bringing about the salvation of many (Eph 2:4–5). Second, the power of God's grace is greater than the power of sin (Rom 5:20). The redemptive work of Christ ensures that grace can and will prevail over sin, leading to the progressive growth of righteousness in individuals.[4]

Third, Mathison observes that Christ's redemptive work on the cross, intended to overcome sin, is an "accomplished fact" (John 19:30).[5] This victory over sin forms the basis for the postmillennial expectation of the progressive triumph of righteousness. Fourth, postmillennialism does not claim that perfection will be attained before the second coming of Christ. Rather, it anticipates a progressive growth of righteousness, similar to the growth seen in individual redemption (Phil 1:6).[6] Thus, objecting to postmillennialism based on the reality of sin overlooks the transformative power of the gospel and the ongoing work of redemption in individuals and societies alike.

---

3. Gentry, *Postmillennialism*, 117.
4. Mathison, *Postmillennialism*, 198.
5. Mathison, *Postmillennialism*, 198.
6. Mathison, *Postmillennialism*, 198–99.

Response to Common Objections

Christian Suffering

The objection that postmillennialism diminishes suffering with Christ typically stems from the perception that it downplays the reality and necessity of suffering in the Christian life. Critics argue that this optimistic view fails to account for the New Testament's emphasis on suffering as a vital aspect of the believer's union with the Lord. However, a closer examination of postmillennialism reveals that it does not negate the reality of suffering but situates it within a broader narrative of redemptive history and gospel advancement. In other words, while recognizing the reality of suffering, postmillennialism maintains an optimistic view that these trials contribute to the ultimate good and progress of humanity under God's redemptive plan (cf. Rom 8:28; 2 Cor 4:17).

Gentry argues that this objection often stems from a "historical pessimism" inherent in all other eschatological systems.[7] These systems emphasize that the church's role is to endure suffering throughout history, with its ultimate glory realized only in the future. For instance, Kim Riddlebarger argues that the church will be destroyed as an influential institution for spreading the gospel, foreseeing a time when every nation will submit to an anti-Christian authority.[8] According to his view, there is no extended period of righteousness within the church's historical progression; instead, it presents a pessimistic eschatology.

Postmillennialists agree that the New Testament highlights suffering as a component of the Christian life; for example, Paul in Rom 8:17 asserts, "If we are children, then heirs—heirs of God and fellow heirs with Christ, provided we suffer with him in order that we may also be glorified with him." Gentry notes that this suffering is contextualized by Paul within the present age of creation's groaning and futility (Rom 8:20, 22).[9] Despite freedom from the law of sin and death (8:2), believers endure physical weaknesses like hunger, illness, injury, and even corporeal death, typical of a fallen world. Paul reflects on his mortal body's limitations (6:12; 8:11), which is subject to corruption and decay (1 Cor 15:53–57).[10]

---

7. Gentry, *He Shall Have Dominion*, 471.

8. Riddlebarger, *Case for Amillennialism*, 127. See also Hendriksen, *More Than Conquerors*.

9. Gentry, *He Shall Have Dominion*, 477.

10. Gentry, *He Shall Have Dominion*, 477.

Gentry also observes that Christians endure suffering due to the pervasive presence of evil in the world, noting that believers lament the sinful inclinations within themselves and others.[11] Paul portrays his internal conflict with sin in Rom 7:21–23 and expresses his distress in 7:24: "Wretched man that I am!" Even amid the advancement of God's kingdom, Christians confront temptations and wrestle with sin (Matt 13:22). The ongoing struggle against worldly desires highlights the enduring nature of suffering. Hence, postmillennialism acknowledges that Christians will suffer with Christ until his return, bearing the burdens of their predecessors, enduring the consequences of original sin, and grappling with mortality itself.[12]

PRACTICAL OBJECTIONS

Failure of the Kingdom

The objection that postmillennialism is false because the current world conditions do not align with its expectations of kingdom growth is another common critique. Critics argue that the visible state of the world, marked by wars, moral decline, and fluctuating Christian influence, undermines the postmillennial vision of a progressively triumphant kingdom of God.[13] However, a thorough examination of postmillennial objections to this argument demonstrates that this objection misunderstands the nature and trajectory of Christ's kingdom.

Gentry highlights the postmillennial view of the kingdom's gradual, mysterious growth, echoing Jesus' parable of the mustard seed (Matt 13:31–32). This parable illustrates how the kingdom begins small but grows to dominate, suggesting that judging its current state as unsuccessful is like condemning a seed for not yet being a fruit-bearing tree.[14] Gentry further notes that the kingdom has witnessed significant growth since the first century, despite early persecution and martyrdom. Today, while sporadic violent persecution persists, it is less widespread than in the early church

---

11. Gentry, *He Shall Have Dominion*, 478.
12. Gentry, *He Shall Have Dominion*, 479.
13. Walvoord, *Millennial Kingdom*, 8–9; Riddlebarger, *Case for Amillennialism*, 281; George Eldon Ladd, "An Historic Premillennial Response," in Clouse, *Meaning of the Millennium*, 143.
14. Gentry, *Postmillennialism*, 117.

period. This points to the historical advancement of the church rather than failure in the kingdom's expansion.[15]

Hal Lindsey's view that events like World War I and II discredit postmillennialism reflects Bahnsen's critique of "newspaper exegesis."[16] Bahnsen argues against interpreting biblical prophecy through contemporary events, noting that temporary setbacks or crises, such as global conflicts or moral decline, do not invalidate the biblical promises of kingdom growth. Just as the delayed return of Christ does not disprove his eventual coming, Bahnsen asserts that current world conditions reported in the news cannot challenge God's sovereignty.[17] Isaiah 46:10, 55:11, and Eph 1:11 affirm that God works all things according to his will, ensuring the kingdom progresses towards its fulfillment as part of his divine plan.

Undermines Watchfulness

Postmillennialism is often charged with diminishing the urgency of being watchful and prepared for Christ's return, with some arguing that it removes the sense of "imminent" expectation central to biblical teachings.[18] However, this objection overlooks the nuanced understanding of biblical watchfulness and the specific implications of postmillennial eschatology. Rather than negating the need for watchfulness, postmillennialism reframes it within the context of active participation in God's redemptive work.[19]

The biblical mandate for watchfulness and preparedness does not inherently demand the doctrine of imminence. Mathison rightly observes that the Greek word translated as "watch" in passages such as Matt 24:42 and 25:13 is γρηγορεῖτε (*grēgoreō*), which literally means to "keep awake." He argues that "we should be actively and obediently serving Christ, watching

---

15. Gentry, *Postmillennialism*, 117–18.

16. Lindsey states, "No self-respecting scholar who looks at the world conditions and the accelerating decline of Christian influence today is a 'postmillennialist.'" Lindsey and Carlson, *Late Great Planet Earth*, 164–65.

17. Bahnsen, *Victory in Jesus*, 72–74. See also Mathison, *Postmillennialism*, 201–2.

18. For example, see Showers, *Maranatha*, 127–53.

19. For a thorough critique against "imminence," see Allis, *Prophecy and the Church*, 167–75. See also Gentry, *He Shall Have Dominion*, 438–42; Grudem, *Systematic Theology*, 1343–58.

ourselves and not the sky (cf. Acts 1:11)."[20] Additionally, texts used to support the doctrine of imminence, such as those in Revelation (1:1, 3; 22:6, 7, 10, 12, 20), do not support this view. As discussed in chapter 6 of this present work, John's prophecies, which point to imminent events, are better understood as referring to Christ's coming in judgment on Jerusalem in the first century rather than his bodily return at the end of the age.[21]

This is not to say that Christ *cannot* come at any moment. Christ *can* come at any time because God sovereignly accomplishes his will in all things (cf. Ps 115:3). As mentioned in chapter 4 of this book, Paul discusses in Rom 11 that not all Jews have embraced Christ, but he anticipates a future where a significant number will come to faith. Therefore, it seems unlikely that Christ will return until the majority of the ethnic Jews turn to Christ. Ultimately, the timing of Christ's return hinges on God's knowledge of when the full number of the gentiles destined for salvation will be complete (Rom 11:25).

BIBLICAL OBJECTIONS

Matthew 7:13–14

> Enter by the narrow gate. For the gate is wide and the way is easy that leads to destruction, and those who enter by it are many. For the gate is narrow and the way is hard that leads to life, and those who find it are few. (Matt 7:13–14)

Matthew 7:13–14, part of the Sermon on the Mount (Matt 5–7), presents Jesus' teachings on righteous living. These verses warn about false prophets (7:15–20) and emphasize the consequences of disregarding his instructions (7:24–27). The Sermon on the Mount urges believers to embody Christian virtues like meekness, mercy, purity, and peacemaking (5:3–12). The passage above is cited in objection to the postmillennial eschatological view, which holds the belief that most of humanity will embrace Christ before his return.[22] Therefore, it is crucial to consider this comment within its appropriate context.

---

20. Mathison, *Postmillennialism*, 205; cf. Danker et al., *Lexicon*, 208.

21. Mathison, *Postmillennialism*, 205

22. Wayne Grudem highlights Matt 7:13–14 as a significant objection to postmillennialism. He argues that Jesus' teaching on the narrow gate and the broad road suggests that only a few will be saved compared to the many who will be lost. Grudem, *Systematic*

B. B. Warfield interprets these verses not as a prophetic statement about the end times, but as a call to ethical living. Jesus contrasts two paths: one demanding ethical rigor (the narrow gate and road) and another of moral laxity (the broad road). The narrow path, challenging yet rewarding, reflects Christ's call to intentional discipleship. In contrast, the broad road offers ease, which is appealing to the masses, but it leads to spiritual and moral ruin.[23] In essence, this is a proverbial statement, not a prediction about the number of people saved or damned at the end of the age.

Mathison concurs, suggesting that Jesus was addressing the prevalent disbelief among Jews during his ministry. He emphasizes that this passage does not comment on the ultimate number of people who will accept or reject Christ but rather on the immediate context of his audience's response. He notes that the Lord's teaching was a direct challenge to the prevailing attitudes and beliefs of his contemporaries.[24] Furthermore, and only a few verses later, Jesus states that "many will come from east and west and recline at table with Abraham, Isaac, and Jacob in the kingdom of heaven" (8:11).[25] This indicates that an enormous number of people from all nations will ultimately embrace the gospel and participate in the blessings of God's kingdom.

Additionally, the sermon's central theme is summarized in Matt 5:48, where Jesus says, "You therefore must be perfect, as your heavenly Father is perfect."[26] The Greek word for "perfect" (τέλειοι, teleioi) does not imply sinlessness or moral flawlessness. Instead, it conveys the idea of "completeness, wholeness, maturity—being all that God wants a person to be."[27] Although this objective is unattainable in this earthly life, it serves as a constant task

---

Theology, 1386.

23. Warfield, *Biblical and Theological Studies*, 338.

24. Davis agrees, stating, "Christ's sayings concerning the narrow door and the narrow gate . . . describe the limited response of the Jews to the earthly ministry of Jesus, and not the ultimate outcome of God's saving purpose." Davis, *Christ's Victorious Kingdom*, 133; Mathison, *Postmillennialism*, 209. See also Wilson, *Heaven Misplaced*, 78–79.

25. Gentry, *Postmillennialism*, 119.

26. Gill notes that the narrow way described by Jesus is seen as difficult and unpopular, attracting few travelers. In contrast, many prefer the wide gates, expansive paths, and bustling crowds. Human nature tends to favor freedom of movement and association with others, even in wrongdoing. Consequently, Christ's path is sparsely populated, with relatively few choosing to walk it and find salvation. Gill, *Exposition of the New Testament*, 1:63.

27. Youngblood, *Dictionary*, 1039.

for followers of Christ to strive for greater spiritual achievements.[28] Thus, Matt 7:13–14 serves as a call to ethical living and intentional discipleship, rather than a prophetic statement about the end times.

Matthew 13:36–39

> Then he left the crowds and went into the house. And his disciples came to him, saying, "Explain to us the parable of the weeds of the field." He answered, "The one who sows the good seed is the Son of Man. The field is the world, and the good seed is the sons of the kingdom. The weeds are the sons of the evil one, and the enemy who sowed them is the devil. The harvest is the end of the age, and the reapers are angels." (Matt 13:36–39)

A common misunderstanding about postmillennialism is the belief that it teaches universal salvation, implying that eventually, all individuals on the planet will be saved. However, this interpretation is incorrect. Postmillennialism actually asserts that there will be widespread gospel success and substantial conversions, but it does not claim universal salvation for every person. This view is grounded in Scripture, which clearly states otherwise (cf. Matt 25:46; Rev 20:15).

Due to their confusion, critics of postmillennialism often point to passages like Matt 13:36–39, which describe the coexistence of the righteous (good seed) and the wicked (weeds) until the end of the age. They argue that this portrayal contradicts the postmillennial expectation of a future era marked by widespread righteousness and prosperity. For instance, Floyd Hamilton states, "The teaching of the parable of the wheat and the tears, Matt. 13, that both the sons of the kingdom and the sons of the evil one are to be in the world right up to the end of the age, clearly contradicts any view of the universality of Christianity throughout the world for a thousand years."[29] However, postmillennialists teach that, despite the worldwide success of the gospel, there will always be a mixture of the righteous and the unrighteous.[30]

Interestingly, Mathison notes that the parable is actually more favorable to a postmillennial interpretation. At the end of the age, Christ returns

---

28. Youngblood, *Dictionary*, 1039.

29. Hamilton, *Basis of Millennial Faith*, 33.

30. Gentry, *He Shall Have Dominion*, 490–92. See also Bahnsen, *Victory in Jesus*, 74–76; Boettner, *Millennium*, 54–57.

to a field predominantly of *wheat*, not a field of *weeds*.[31] This aligns with the postmillennial view that the kingdom of God will grow significantly and have a profound influence on the world, even though evil will still exist until the final judgment.

Likewise, Gentry observes that the parable depicts the world as God's field, where he intends to plant the wheat.[32] In Matt 13:24, God sows good seed in his field, identified as the world (13:38). However, an adversary—the devil—intervenes by sowing weeds (representing the wicked) among the wheat (13:39). Gentry argues that the point of the parable is that weeds will be found among the predominant *wheat*; the weeds are the "intruders," not the wheat.[33] This indicates that while evil exists, it does so among the widespread presence of the righteous, aligning with the postmillennial expectation of gospel dominance.

Luke 18:7–8

> And will not God give justice to his elect, who cry to him day and night? Will he delay long over them? I tell you, he will give justice to them speedily. Nevertheless, when the Son of Man comes, will he find faith on earth? (Luke 18:7–8)

Non-postmillennialists often seek to undermine the system by invoking the question posed in Luke 18:8, "When the Son of Man comes, will he find faith on earth?" Boettner points out that these critics typically interpret this question to imply a negative answer.[34] For instance, Stanley J. Grenz argues that it functions rhetorically, reflecting the Lord's concern that faith may wane due to the prolonged delay of his second coming.[35] However, the question itself does not inherently necessitate a negative response, neither is it strictly rhetorical.

Gentry contends that such objections miss the intended focus of Christ's inquiry. The passage, he argues, primarily addresses the persistence of fervent prayer rather than the future existence of Christianity.[36]

---

31. Mathison, *Postmillennialism*, 211.
32. Gentry, *Postmillennialism*, 120.
33. Gentry, *Postmillennialism*, 120.
34. Boettner, *Millennium*, 47.
35. Grenz, *Millennial Maze*, 87.
36. Gentry, *He Shall Have Dominion*, 493–94.

The Greek term for "faith" (τὴν πίστιν, *tēn pistin*) in this context includes a definite article, referring specifically to the faith previously mentioned—the faith of the persistent widow.[37] "And he told them a parable to the effect that they ought always to pray and not lose heart" (Luke 18:1). Christ's teaching aims not to speculate on the continuity of Christian faith in the future, but rather to encourage steadfastness in prayer among his disciples. In essence, the purpose of this parable is ethical rather than eschatological.

Furthermore, Gentry argues that objections based on the grammar of Jesus' question are misguided. The form of the question in Greek does not inherently imply a negative answer; it is not strictly rhetorical.[38] Mathison concurs, noting that the Greek construction leaves the answer undetermined, neither necessitating a negative nor a positive response.[39] Thus, attempts to discredit postmillennialism using Luke 18:8 distort the ethical thrust of Christ's teaching on persistent prayer into an unwarranted speculation about the future of Christianity.

2 Thessalonians 2:1–4

> Now concerning the coming of our Lord Jesus Christ and our being gathered together to him, we ask you, brothers, not to be quickly shaken in mind or alarmed, either by a spirit or a spoken word, or a letter seeming to be from us, to the effect that the day of the Lord has come. Let no one deceive you in any way. For that day will not come, unless the rebellion comes first, and the man of lawlessness is revealed, the son of destruction, who opposes and exalts himself against every so-called god or object of worship, so that he takes his seat in the temple of God, proclaiming himself to be God. (2 Thess 2:1–4)

Non-postmillennialists use 2 Thess 2:1–4 to challenge postmillennialism, arguing that Paul's depiction of the "man of lawlessness" and apostasy foretells future events *immediately* preceding Christ's second coming.[40]

---

37. Gentry, *He Shall Have Dominion*, 494.

38. In his writing, Gentry explains that in Luke 18:8, the absence of specific interrogative particles like *ou* (οὐ) for affirmative answers or *me* (μήτι, *meti*) for negative responses leaves the implied answer to the question ambiguous. The Greek word *ara* (ἄρα) used here only conveys a tone of suspense or impatience in interrogation, rather than indicating a definitive answer. Gentry, *He Shall Have Dominion*, 494.

39. Mathison, *Postmillennialism*, 212–13.

40. Thomas Ice, "The Great Tribulation Is Future: The New Testament," in Ice and

They view this passage as predicting a future period of severe apostasy of the church, the rise of an antichrist figure, and a final tribulation before Christ's bodily return.[41] However, this author posits that 2 Thess 2:1–4 does not pertain to the second advent, but that it refers to Christ's coming in judgment against the Jews in AD 70.

In 1 Thessalonians, Paul addresses the Thessalonian church's concerns about the second coming of Christ and the fate of the deceased believers (1 Thess 4:13–18). Shortly after, the Thessalonians became confused about the timing of the day of the Lord, possibly thinking it had already occurred (1 Thess 5:1–6). Paul reassures them in 2 Thessalonians by clarifying misunderstandings about the sequence of events before Christ's return.

In 2 Thess 2:1–3, Paul explains that the day of the Lord will not come until two things happen: first, apostasy ἀποστασία (*apostasia*, or rebellion), which historically occurred with the Jewish revolt against Rome within two decades of Paul's writing; and second, the revelation of the man of lawlessness.[42] This figure, according to Paul, is someone alive during his time and will be revealed before the day of the Lord (2:6).

Moreover, 2 Thess 2:6 states that the lawlessness (or the man of lawlessness) is currently being restrained. Nero Caesar, historically, was known for his lawlessness and cruelty, including the persecution of Christians.[43] His reign fits the description of one who opposes God and exalts himself (2:4).[44] Nero's rule, characterized by unprecedented persecution of Christians and general cruelty, ended with his death in AD 68, during the Jewish war. This period was marked by significant turmoil and judgment upon

---

Gentry, *Great Tribulation*, 97; MacArthur, *1 and 2 Thessalonians*, 263–74. For a thorough interpretation of 1 and 2 Thessalonians from a dispensational perspective, see Hiebert, *1 and 2 Thessalonians*.

41. Poole, *Commentary*, 3:758–61.

42. The Greek word ἀποστασία, translated as "apostasy," denotes rebellion, encompassing both political and religious defiance. Gentry contends that it specifically pertains to the Jewish uprising against Roman authority. D. Edmond Hiebert also observes that in classical Greek, the word ἀποστασία signifies political or military rebellion. However, he himself suggests that in this context, it refers to the Christian church. Gentry, *He Shall Have Dominion*, 392–93; Hiebert, *1 and 2 Thessalonians*, 331. See also Mathison, *Postmillennialism*, 231; Danker et al., *Lexicon*, 208.

43. Suetonius, *Nero*, 16, 26, 28–29, 33–35.

44. Nero had a statue in Rome, designed for worship, equal in size to the statue of Mars. Robinson, *Redating*, 236; Quintern, "Neronic Date," 112.

Israel, leading up to the destruction of Jerusalem and the Second Temple in AD 70.[45]

Thus, Paul's letters to the Thessalonians serve to alleviate their anxieties concerning Christ's return and the timing of eschatological events. Initially comforted in 1 Thessalonians by the sequence preceding Christ's return, the Thessalonians later grew apprehensive, fearing they had missed the day of the Lord. Paul's clarification in 2 Thessalonians highlights the necessity of specific preconditions—such as apostasy and the revelation of the man of lawlessness—prior to the day of the Lord's manifestation. Nero Caesar's rule exemplifies defiance against God, characterized by intense persecution of Christians that led to the martyrdom of both Peter and Paul.[46]

2 Timothy 3:1–4, 13

> But understand this, that in the last days there will come times of difficulty. For people will be lovers of self, lovers of money, proud, arrogant, abusive, disobedient to their parents, ungrateful, unholy, heartless, unappeasable, slanderous, without self-control, brutal, not loving good, treacherous, reckless, swollen with conceit, lovers of pleasure rather than lovers of God. . . . Evil people and impostors will go on from bad to worse, deceiving and being deceived. (2 Tim 3:1–4, 13)

Critics frequently cite 2 Tim 3 as evidence against postmillennialism's optimistic view. They interpret this passage as depicting a continuous increase in evil throughout history, arguing that this precludes the possibility of a golden age of Christianity prior to Christ's return.[47] However, this objection arises from a misunderstanding of the passage's context.

First, the immediate context shows that Paul is addressing Timothy concerning the conditions he would face in his own time (3:10). Paul references Timothy's experiences and his own teaching, conduct, and persecutions. This indicates that Paul is speaking to the immediate historical context rather than providing a broad, sweeping prophecy about the entire Church Age. This passage does not suggest a linear historical decline, but

---

45. Josephus, *Jewish War*, 5–6.
46. Gentry, *Beast of Revelation*, 66–67.
47. Lindsey and Carlson, *Late Great Planet Earth*, 120–21, 171; Riddlebarger, *Case for Amillennialism*, 262.

rather highlights specific instances where evil individuals will morally deteriorate: "Evil people and impostors will go on from bad to worse" (3:13).[48]

Second, the Greek term καιροὶ (*kairoi*), translated as "times" or "seasons," implies periodic, recurrent instances of difficulty rather than a single, unbroken trajectory of moral decline.[49] Paul acknowledges that these challenging seasons will occur but does not suggest that they will dominate the entire Church Age. History supports this interpretation, as the church has experienced cycles of persecution and revival, decline, and reformation. This cyclical pattern aligns with the concept of καιροὶ, emphasizing periods of both hardship and flourishing.

Third, Paul's statement in 2 Tim 3:13 that "evil people and impostors will go on from bad to worse, deceiving and being deceived" must be understood in light of verse 9, where he asserts that "they will not get very far, for their folly will be plain to all." This suggests a limitation on the extent and impact of evil, indicating that while deception and immorality may intensify in certain contexts, they will ultimately be exposed and curtailed.[50] Therefore, when interpreted contextually, 2 Tim 3 does not support the critique of postmillennialism based on the continuous growth of evil, but rather addresses practical pastoral issues Timothy faced in his time.

SUMMARY

This chapter has addressed key objections to postmillennialism, focusing on theological, practical, and biblical critiques. Theological objections, such as the inherent sinfulness of humanity and the necessity of Christian suffering, were examined through the insights of Gentry and Mathison. They argue that the transformative power of the gospel and the progressive growth of righteousness counter the objection that sin precludes widespread gospel success. Similarly, postmillennialism does not negate the reality of suffering but situates it within a broader narrative of redemptive history, anticipating eventual redemption despite the presence of evil.

Practical objections, including the perceived failure of the kingdom and the undermining of watchfulness, were also considered. The gradual, mysterious growth of Christ's kingdom, likened to the parable of the mustard seed, demonstrates historical advancement despite temporary

---

48. Gentry, *Postmillennialism*, 122.
49. Gentry, *Postmillennialism*, 122. See also Danker et al., *Lexicon*, 497.
50. Gentry, *Postmillennialism*, 123.

setbacks. Postmillennialism reframes the concept of watchfulness as active participation in God's redemptive work, focusing on personal faithfulness rather than imminent expectation. Biblical objections, including interpretations of Matt 7:13–14, Matt 13:36–39, Luke 18:7–8, 2 Thess 2:1–4, and 2 Tim 3:1–4, 13, were contextualized and shown to support a postmillennial view.[51]

---

51. Joel R. Beeke and Paul M. Smalley write, "We believe that a convincing argument can be made that the Holy Scriptures teach inaugurated millennialism, with the expectation that Christ will empower the church so that many people will be saved, but not that the church will have a generally preeminent spiritual influence in society." They argue that there will be "no era of peace for the church" prior to the second coming of Christ, employing many of the aforementioned arguments to support this conclusion. Beeke and Smalley, *Reformed Systematic Theology*, 902–4.

Chapter Nine

Response to Specific Critiques

CRITIQUES BY SEXTON

Jeremy Sexton highlights a fundamental question at the heart of eschatological debates: "When will earth experience the worldwide peace, piety, and prosperity anticipated in Scripture—before the second coming or after?"[1] According to postmillennialism, these conditions will emerge before Christ's return. Since Sexton critiques this view for lacking scriptural foundation, this chapter will focus on briefly addressing his concerns with pivotal texts such as Matt 28:18–20, 1 Cor 15:24–28, and key passages in Revelation.

Response: Matthew 28:18–20

Sexton's critique of Matt 28:18–20 revolves around the interpretation of the Great Commission and its implications for postmillennialism. He argues that the command to "disciple all nations" does not necessarily imply the conversion of entire nations or peoples to the Christian faith. Instead, he suggests that this directive involves spreading the gospel and making disciples among all ethnic groups without guaranteeing that every individual or nation will fully embrace Christianity before the second coming.[2]

Sexton's interpretation of Matt 28:18–20 raises important questions about the extent of the church's mission to "disciple all nations." However, a closer look at the passage in light of Christ's absolute authority and the

---

1. Sexton, "Postmillennialism," 554.
2. Sexton, "Postmillennialism," 555–58.

comprehensive mandate he provides offers a strong support for the postmillennial perspective. First, the assertion that Christ has been given "all authority in heaven and on earth" highlights the ultimate power and reach of his kingship (28:18). This is not merely a spiritual or abstract authority but one that extends over all creation.[3] The significance of this authority is crucial as it implies that Christ's commands are not just aspirational but are backed by the power to ensure their fulfillment.

Second, the command to "make disciples of all nations ... teaching them to observe all that I have commanded you" extends beyond mere evangelism, involving a deep, transformative education in Christ's ways as conveyed by the Greek term διδάσκοντες (*didaskontes*), meaning "teaching."[4] This instruction seeks to ethically transform individuals who, in turn, impact the broader societal structure by aligning it with the values of the kingdom of God. However, this mission does not imply that every individual will convert, as depicted in the parable of the weeds (13:24–30), which illustrates that the kingdom will comprise both believers and unbelievers, coexisting until the end of the age.[5] The presence of both belief and unbelief throughout the kingdom's expansion reflects a realistic outlook on historical processes. Ultimately, the kingdom is expected to grow significantly before the second coming of Christ (cf. 13:31–32).

Third, the promise of Jesus, "I am with you always, to the end of the age" (28:20), provides divine assurance that the mission will not be in vain but will be upheld by Christ's continual presence and support.[6] This indicates a divine endorsement and guarantee of success in the mission which aligns with postmillennialism's optimistic outlook on the extent of the kingdom's influence prior to the second coming of Christ.[7] In light of these elements, Sexton's critique may overlook the depth of the mandate given in the Great Commission.

---

3. As noted in chapter 4, the Greek term ἐξουσία (*exousia*), meaning "authority," denotes the right to govern, the power to take action, and the authority to rule. Bruce points out that ἐξουσία encompasses all types of authority, representing control over all resources essential for the progression of God's kingdom. Alexander Balmain Bruce, "Synoptic Gospels," in Nicoll, *Expositor's Greek Testament*, 1:339.

4. Danker et al., *Lexicon*, 240–41.

5. Mathison, *Postmillennialism*, 211; Murray, *Puritan Hope*, xx.

6. Chilton, *Paradise Restored*, 213.

7. Mathison, *Postmillennialism*, 116.

Response to Specific Critiques

Response: 1 Corinthians 15:24–28

Sexton challenges the postmillennial view by arguing that 1 Cor 15:24–28 does not support the idea that Christ will progressively subdue all his enemies, except death, before his return. He contends that Paul describes the destruction of Christ's enemies as occurring at "the end," implying a *simultaneous* defeat rather than *progressive* subjugation.[8] Sexton bases this on the Greek conjunction ὅταν (when), used twice in adjacent temporal clauses, which he interprets as emphasizing a definitive, concurrent event: the destruction of all rule, authority, and power, followed by the delivery of the kingdom to the Father. He states,

> Paul temporally locates the action of "he shall destroy" at "the end." Note that τὸ τέλος ("the end") is modified by two adjacent temporal clauses, each one beginning with ὅταν ("when") followed by a subjunctive verb: ὅταν παραδιδῷ ... ὅταν καταργήσῃ ("when he shall deliver ... when he shall destroy"). Both actions of this double-sided event—the destruction of every rule, authority, and power and the delivery of the kingdom to the Father—will take place "when" "the end" arrives. The aorist subjunctive καταργήσῃ ("he shall destroy"), whose aspect is perfective, describes an event that will occur as a whole, in its entirety, from beginning to end, "when" "the end" comes.[9]

However, James A. Brooks and Carlton L. Winberry argue that the subjunctive with ὅταν and related temporal conjunctions often indicates an indefinite and future-oriented action, suggesting a degree of fluidity in the timing and realization of events. They note,

> The subjunctive with ὅταν, ἐπάν, or ἡνύκα (all of which mean "whenever") and with ἕως, ἕως οὗ, ἕως ὅτου, ἄχρι, ἄχρι οὗ, μέχρυ(ς), μέχρι(ς) οὗ, or ὡς ἄν (all of which mean "until") is used in clauses where the temporal element is indefinite and implies uncertainty as to realization.[10]

This grammatical insight supports a view that, while the ultimate outcomes (i.e., the subjugation of all enemies and the defeat of death) are indeed definitive, their realization may not be as immediate or as concurrent as Sexton suggests. The subjunctive with ὅταν, indicating an indefinite timing,

---

8. Sexton, "Postmillennialism," 558–62.
9. Sexton, "Postmillennialism," 559.
10. Brooks and Winberry, *Syntax of New Testament Greek*, 111.

leaves room for a more gradual unfolding of these eschatological events, which aligns with postmillennialism.

Response: Revelation 20:7–10

Sexton further critiques postmillennialism by pointing out what he considers to be a significant inconsistency in the postmillennial interpretation of Rev 20:7–10. He argues that, according to this passage, Satan will deceive the nations at the end of the millennium, leading to a widespread rebellion against God. This scenario, he claims, contradicts the postmillennial expectation that the world will be largely Christianized and discipled by the time of Christ's return.[11]

Sexton observes that Gary North, a postmillennialist, acknowledges this issue and attempts to resolve it by suggesting that the rebellion will arise from within a superficially Christianized world—one that is externally obedient but internally rebellious.[12] However, Sexton criticizes this explanation, arguing that it fails to align with the postmillennial expectation of comprehensive discipleship as envisioned in passages like Matt 28:18–20. He contends that if postmillennialists were consistent they would have to admit that Satan's deception will affect all nations, leading to a world filled with reprobates, which undermines the postmillennial hope for a victorious and expansive kingdom of God.[13]

It is important to note that the "apostasy" is said to occur *after* the millennium, not within it: "When the thousand years are ended" (Rev 20:7).[14] Moreover, North's interpretation is more reasonable when, again, considered alongside the parable of the weeds (Matt 13:24–30; 36–43). This parable suggests that history reveals a progressive separation between the saved and the lost, with the kingdom of God containing both genuine believers and unbelievers.[15] It indicates that, while the kingdom is primarily made up of wheat (believers), there will still be a significant presence of weeds (unbelievers).

---

11. Sexton, "Postmillennialism," 563–65. See also Riddlebarger, *Case for Amillennialism*, 249–50.

12. Sexton, "Postmillennialism," 563–65; North, *Dominion and Common Grace*, xv–xvi.

13. Sexton, "Postmillennialism," 565.

14. Gentry, *He Shall Have Dominion*, 514.

15. North, *Dominion and Common Grace*, 66.

Response to Specific Critiques

The parable of the weeds, along with the parable of the net (13:47–49), teaches that both groups will coexist within the kingdom until the end of the age. At the second coming, there will be a final separation, with unbelievers facing judgment and being expelled from the kingdom (cf. Rev 20:7–15). Importantly, this parable refers to the kingdom of God as a whole, not just the church, with the "field" representing the "world" (Matt 13:38). The angels, acting as reapers, are instructed to allow the weeds to grow alongside the wheat until the final harvest for the sake of the elect (wheat). This coexistence highlights the nature of the kingdom, where both the regenerate and unregenerate share the same world until the end.

Additionally, placed between the parable of the weeds and the parable of the net are the parables of the mustard seed and the leaven (13:31–33). Both parables explain that the kingdom of heaven starts small, like a mustard seed or leaven, but grows gradually and eventually becomes vast and influential (see chapter 4). This is reminiscent of Old Testament prophetic themes, such as the stone from heaven that grew into a great mountain (Dan 2:31–35, 44) and the water flowing from the temple that widened and deepened into a mighty river (Ezek 47:1–9).[16]

Sexton also challenges how postmillennialists interpret Rev 20:8. He argues that "postmillennialists simply gloss over the comprehensive force of the phrase 'the nations that are in the four corners of the earth' and divert attention to the qualifier 'whose number is like the sand of the sea' (Rev 20:8)."[17] However, the symbolic adversaries mentioned in verse 8, "Gog and Magog" from Ezek 38 and 39, are often regarded in Jewish texts as the "final major enemies of Israel."[18] This verse simply indicates that there will be a significant number of those who are rebelling against the kingdom of God. Yet, as Gentry notes, the very notion of this revolt suggests Christianity's prior dominance.[19]

Sexton then states,

> The earth will be littered with deceived nations and an uncountable number of rebels that he must subdue and destroy at his coming. This does not fit with the postmillennial tenet that Christ will

---

16. Davis, *Christ's Victorious Kingdom*, 49.
17. Sexton, "Postmillennialism," 564.
18. Keener, *Background Commentary*, 771.
19. Gentry, *He Shall Have Dominion*, 515.

subdue and destroy every rule, authority, and power during his heavenly reign, so that death is the only enemy left at his return.[20]

Nevertheless, Sexton's concern that Christ must subdue and destroy all enemies before his return does not conflict with postmillennialism. The final rebellion is part of the process where Christ's enemies are ultimately defeated. Christ's kingdom will expand and subdue nations progressively, but this does not negate the possibility of a final, desperate rebellion by Satan, which Christ will decisively crush at his return (Rev 20:7–10).[21] This sequence of events is consistent with the gradual and ultimate victory depicted in 1 Cor 15:24–26, where Christ reigns until he has put all his enemies under his feet.

Response: Revelation 19:17–21

Sexton critiques the postmillennial interpretation of Rev 19:11–21 by arguing that the preterist view, which interprets this passage as referring to Christ's judgment on Jerusalem in AD 70, is flawed. He contends that postmillennialists overlook the universal scope of the battle described in the passage, where Christ is depicted as smiting "the nations" and defeating "the kings of the earth with their armies." Sexton argues that the text clearly refers to a worldwide judgment, not a localized event in Jerusalem.[22]

However, this author would argue that Sexton himself misses a key aspect of the text: the judgment specifically targets the beast and the false prophet. The passage states,

> And I saw the beast and the kings of the earth with their armies gathered to make war against him who was sitting on the horse and against his army. And the beast was captured, and with it the false prophet who in its presence had done the signs by which he deceived those who had received the mark of the beast and those who worshiped its image. These two were thrown alive into the lake of fire that burns with sulfur. (Rev 19:19–20)

---

20. Sexton, "Postmillennialism," 565.

21. Again, it should be noted that the apostasy is stated to occur *after* the millennium, not *during* the millennium. Gentry states, "Revelation 20:7–10 teaches only that *after the end of the 'millennium'* and *just before the end of history* some will fall away and revolt against the prevailing Christian culture." *He Shall Have Dominion*, 514 (emphasis original).

22. Sexton, "Postmillennialism," 567–68.

RESPONSE TO SPECIFIC CRITIQUES

In chapter 6 of this study, it is explained that the beast has a dual identity, representing both Rome in general and Nero specifically. The false prophet, mentioned in Rev 19, is portrayed as a lesser beast that appears elsewhere like a "lamb" (Rev 13:11), which, in this context, likely alludes to Israel's temple sacrifices where lambs were a common offering (cf. Lev 4:32–33).[23] This interpretation is reinforced by the fact that the other lamb mentioned in Revelation is the Lamb of God, who was crucified by the religious leaders of Israel in cooperation with Rome (Matt 20:18–19; 26:59, 66; 27:1).[24]

Moreover, the false prophet in Rev 19:20 is closely tied to the devil and the first beast (Rev 16:13; 20:10). Gentry points out that in Scripture, false prophecy is typically associated with the covenant community and often has a religious dimension. He observes that among the Jews, prophecy was closely linked to the high priesthood.[25] For instance, Josephus[26] and Philo[27] both connect the gift of prophecy with the high priesthood. Thus, the false prophet likely represents the religious leaders of Israel, particularly the high priesthood.

Furthermore, Gentry contends that the vision in Rev 19:17–21 is central to the book's overarching theme, particularly the judgment of the apostate Jews responsible for Christ's crucifixion, as highlighted in Rev 1:7 (discussed in chapter 6).[28] The phrase "those who pierced him" from Zech 12:10 refers to the Jewish people involved in Jesus' crucifixion, linking this vision to the destruction of Jerusalem. Additionally, Gentry explains that in the Old Testament, "coming with the clouds" frequently symbolizes divine judgment (cf. Pss 18:7–15; 104:3; Isa 19:1; Joel 2:1–2).[29]

The imagery in Rev 19, including the horses in battle, sharp swords, and the treading of the winepress, portrays Christ's triumphant judgment and the complete defeat of his enemies, with Babylon-Jerusalem being the

---

23. Terry interprets this lesser beast as representing the procurators or governors, such as Pilate (Matt 27:2, 11, 27). In contrast, Wilson understands the lesser beast to symbolize the religious leaders of Israel. Terry, *Apocalypse of John*, 175–76; Wilson, *Commentary*, 154.

24. Gentry, *Divorce of Israel*, 2:1091.

25. Gentry, *Divorce of Israel*, 2:1091–92.

26. Josephus, *Antiquities*, 5.2.10; 6.6.3.

27. Philo, *Special Laws*, 4.36 §192, in *Philo in Ten Volumes*, 3–156.

28. Gentry, *Divorce of Israel*, 2:1484. For more information regarding the theme of Revelation, see Gentry, *Before Jerusalem Fell*, 121–32; Quintern, "Neronic Date," 76–82.

29. Gentry, *Before Jerusalem Fell*, 123.

city destined for this destruction.[30] Therefore, while Sexton argues for a global interpretation of the battle in Rev 19, a closer examination reveals that the passage targets specific entities—namely, the beast and the false prophet—within the context of first-century events, particularly the judgment on Jerusalem. Interpreting Rev 19 as depicting a battle of global scope is unwarranted.

SUMMARY

This chapter has addressed the critiques of Jeremy Sexton against postmillennialism, focusing on key biblical texts. The chapter examined Sexton's interpretations of Matt 28:18–20, 1 Cor 15:24–28, and Revelation, challenging his assertions by highlighting the scriptural foundation for a postmillennial perspective. It offers a rebuttal to Sexton's critiques while emphasizing the comprehensive authority of Christ, the progressive nature of his reign, and the eschatological consistency within the postmillennial framework. Ultimately, the chapter argues that Sexton's critiques do not sufficiently undermine the validity of postmillennialism.

---

30. Gentry, *Divorce of Israel*, 2:1485–86.

Chapter Ten

Final Remarks

IMPLICATIONS OF POSTMILLENNIALISM

Postmillennialism emphasizes the belief that Christ will return after a significant period of righteousness and peace, referred to as the "millennium." Central to this view is the Great Commission, where Christians are commanded to "go therefore and make disciples of all nations" (Matt 28:19). This mandate, by its very nature, involves actively engaging in societal structures, including governmental institutions, "teaching them to observe all that [Christ has] commanded" (28:20). This command implies a broad influence on societal norms, ethics, and laws. Since governments play a crucial role in shaping and enforcing these aspects, engaging with governmental institutions is seen as part of fulfilling this mandate.

Wayne Grudem rightly argues that the church should refrain from using physical violence to advance the kingdom of God. He advocates instead for Christians to defend their church communities against violence, noting that Jesus instructed his followers to carry a sword for defense (Luke 22:36).[1] Grudem also observes that seeking to influence civil government to align with biblical principles is scripturally supported (cf. Matt 6:10; 14:4; Acts 24:25; 1 Tim 2:1–4). Throughout the Old Testament, prophets condemn both Israel and pagan societies for moral failings (cf. Deut 9:5; Isa 13–23; Ezek 25–32). Grudem cites 1 Pet 2:14, affirming that civil governments are established by God to punish evil and to commend good.[2]

---

1. Grudem, *Systematic Theology*, 1100.

2. Grudem, *Systematic Theology*, 1102. See also Grudem, *Politics According to the Bible*, 55–76.

Contrary to the notion that the world is under Satan's dominion, postmillennialism emphasizes the Scriptural teaching that Satan is bound with respect to deceiving the nations (Rev 20:2–3). Jesus declared, "All authority in heaven and on earth has been given to me" (Matt 28:18), highlighting the inseparability of his reign over both the spiritual and earthly realms. Consequently, Christians are called to transform their nations through the teachings of Christ.

The apostle Paul also addresses the role of government, stating that "there is no authority except from God, and those that exist have been instituted by God" (Rom 13:1). Any objection stating that Christians should not be actively involved in the discipling of their government because God's sovereignly acts according to his own counsel, implying that Christians' involvement is unnecessary since God ultimately selects the government and authorities, should be rejected. While it is true that God is sovereign over all (Ps 115:3), including the selection of government and authorities, it does not negate the responsibility of Christians to engage in the world actively.[3]

This principle is evident in the doctrine of salvation: God is sovereign in the salvation of individuals, knowing from before the foundations of the earth who would be predestined to eternal life (Eph 1:4–5, Rom 8:29–30). However, God uses his church as the means to accomplish his sovereign plan. As Paul writes, "How, then, can they call on the one they have not believed in? And how can they believe in the one of whom they have not heard? And how can they hear without someone preaching to them?" (Rom 10:14). Therefore, while government functions as an instrument ordained by God to maintain order and justice, the church is called to instruct all nations to abide by his commandments. These two must work together, reinforcing the postmillennial view that societal and governmental engagement is crucial for advancing God's kingdom "on earth as it is in heaven" (Matt 6:10).

Today, Christians who attempt to implement Christian values in government are labeled as "Christian nationalists." While it is not the intention of this book to offer a comprehensive argument for or against Christian nationalism, it is worth briefly mentioning as the postmillennial hope may be reflected in this concept. According to Stephen Wolfe, "Christian nationalism is a totality of national action, consisting of civil laws and social

---

3. R. J. Rushdoony argues, "Christian political action is necessary, towards making the state again a Christian state, and its actions conform with the law of God." Rushdoony, *God's Plan for Victory*, 22.

customs, conducted by a Christian nation as a Christian nation, in order to procure for itself both earthly and heavenly good in Christ."[4] This form of nationalism is not confined to any particular nation or ethnicity; rather, it is a natural fruit of postmillennialism. The ideology of Christian nationalism can be traced back to the early settlers of the United States, who aimed to establish a society grounded in their Christian beliefs. The founding of the United States as a distinctly Christian nation serves as a prime example of this concept in action.

FOUNDATIONS OF A CHRISTIAN NATION

The roots of the Christian foundations in the United States can be traced back to significant religious and political upheavals in England, beginning with Henry VIII's break from the Roman Catholic Church and his establishment of the Church of England. Henry's breakaway was primarily due to his desire for a male heir, his personal infatuation with Anne Boleyn, and his frustration with Pope Clement VII's refusal to annul his marriage to Catherine of Aragon.[5] The 1534 Act of Supremacy declared the English monarch as the supreme head of the Church of England, effectively severing England's ties with the Roman Catholic Church and marking the beginning of state-controlled Protestantism.[6]

The death of Henry VIII in 1547 was followed by the brief reign of the young Edward VI, during which Protestant reforms gained momentum. However, Edward's premature death in 1553 led to the ascension of Mary I, famously known as "Bloody Mary," who sought to restore Catholicism and persecuted Protestant dissenters. Many Puritans, like John Cotton, were exiled or fled to the New World during this period to escape religious persecution.[7]

After the death of Bloody Mary, Queen Elizabeth I's reign (1558–1603) brought a degree of religious stability through the Elizabethan Religious Settlement, which established the Church of England as a blend of Catholic and Protestant practices. However, tensions persisted, especially with the growing Puritan movement. Elizabeth invited the Puritans to return

4. Wolfe, *Case for Christian Nationalism*, 9.

5. MacCulloch, *Reformation*, 194.

6. For a comprehensive study of the Reformation in England, see D'Aubigné, *Reformation in England*.

7. Benge and Pickowicz, *American Puritans*, 2.

to England but insisted on royal authority in appointing bishops, a point of contention for those seeking greater autonomy in church governance.[8] Her policies were more about enforcing religious conformity within the established Church of England rather than actively inviting dissenters who had left.

During Elizabeth's reign, separatist Puritans known as Pilgrims sought refuge in the New World, bringing with them the Geneva Bible and a desire for religious autonomy. King James I's ascension further strained relations, as he opposed Puritanism and centralized control over religious practice. At the Hampton Court Conference in 1604, some leading Puritans had a chance to present to the king their ideas for change in the Church of England. However, James dismissed most of their opinions. He consented only on one point: he was willing to commission a new translation of the scriptures.[9]

Thus, King James commissioned the King James Version of the Bible in 1611 to assert royal authority and promote Anglican orthodoxy. He was concerned about the anti-monarchical annotations in the Geneva Bible, which he viewed as seditious and promoting resistance to the throne. The commissioning of the KJV was also an attempt to unify the various religious factions under a common Bible. However, he was unwilling to yield any further significant changes to the Church of England. The ceremonies, the prayer book, and the bishops were to remain unchanged.[10]

In 1611, James dissolved Parliament so that he could rule England without it. Some in the Puritan movement grew impatient for change in the church. Many Puritans sought refuge in the Netherlands, but, fearing assimilation and cultural loss, they ultimately sought a new homeland where they could establish a society based on their religious ideals. In 1620, a group of Puritans, known as the Pilgrims, embarked on the Mayflower journey to Plymouth, Massachusetts, seeking religious freedom and the opportunity to worship without interference. This marked the beginning of Puritan migration to America, with subsequent waves of settlers establishing colonies throughout New England, including Massachusetts Bay Colony, Connecticut, Rhode Island, and New Hampshire.

The mid-seventeenth century witnessed further religious and political upheaval. Following in the footsteps of his father, Charles I was determined

---

8. Benge and Pickowicz, *American Puritans*, 3.
9. Shelley and Shelley, *Church History*, 346.
10. Shelley and Shelley, *Church History*, 346.

to put his father's theories about the divine right of kings into practice. Charles's reign was marked by severe religious and political tensions, primarily fueled by his and Archbishop William Laud's attempts to enforce uniform Anglican worship across his kingdoms. Laud's stringent policies, including his efforts to impose the English Book of Common Prayer on the Scottish church, deeply alienated many of his subjects and escalated dissent.[11] This religious policy, combined with Charles's autocratic governance style, led to a significant estrangement from the increasingly powerful Parliament, igniting a series of conflicts that eventually sparked the English Civil War.[12]

Oliver Cromwell emerged as a pivotal figure during this period of turmoil. Leading the Parliamentary forces with staunch Puritan zeal, Cromwell's leadership was instrumental in the overthrow and execution of Charles I. During these tumultuous times, the Puritan theologian John Owen served as Cromwell's chaplain, accompanying him on the military campaign in Ireland in 1649. Throughout the Interregnum that followed, Cromwell imposed strict Puritan morals across England, profoundly influencing the religious and political climate of both Britain and its colonies.[13]

The victory was short-lived as the restoration of the monarchy under Charles II in 1660 marked a reversal for dissenting groups. The Act of Uniformity in 1662 not only led to the ejection of nearly two-thousand Puritan ministers from the Church of England but also enforced strict adherence to the Book of Common Prayer across England. While not all Puritans who migrated were separatists desiring to split from the Church of England, many still sought a new life in America due to the hostile religious environment in England.[14]

The arrival of the Puritans in America was a pivotal moment in both religious history and the development of democratic principles. Driven by religious persecution and seeking a haven to practice their faith according to their beliefs, the Puritans played a significant role in shaping the American colonies and ultimately influencing the founding principles of

---

11. In 1638, the English court attempted to enforce the Book of Common Prayer on the Reformed Church of Scotland. This imposition sparked a Scottish revolt against the government of Charles I, ultimately triggering the Wars of the Three Kingdoms. MacCulloch, *All Things Made New*, 147.

12. Ferguson et al., *Church History 101*, 83.

13. Gribben, *Introduction to John Owen*, 35–36.

14. Ferguson et al., *Church History*, 84.

the United States Constitution.[15] The Puritans brought with them a strong sense of community, hard work ethic, and a deeply religious worldview.

They established tightly knit communities governed by principles rooted in Calvinist theology, emphasizing individual piety and communal responsibility. Puritan towns were organized around congregational churches, with local governance closely intertwined with religious leadership. Central to Puritan society was the concept of the covenant, both with God and among individuals within the community. This covenantal theology emphasized mutual obligations and communal welfare, laying the groundwork for early democratic principles and self-governance.[16]

Many of the Puritans were postmillennialists (see chapter 1) who greatly influenced the development of democratic principles and constitutional ideas. The Puritan emphasis on individual conscience, collective decision-making, and rule of law shaped colonial governance and contributed to the emergence of representative institutions.[17] The Mayflower Compact of 1620, signed aboard the ship before the Pilgrims disembarked, exemplified early democratic principles by establishing a self-governing agreement based on the consent of the governed. This document laid the groundwork for later colonial charters and constitutions.[18]

CONCLUSION

The purpose of this book has been to present and defend the postmillennial view of Christian eschatology, drawing significantly from the works of Kenneth L. Gentry Jr. and Keith A. Mathison, both leading proponents of this perspective. The central thesis is that Scripture portrays the gospel, empowered by the Holy Spirit, as ultimately prevailing among diverse peoples and nations, leading to an extended period of righteousness and

---

15. At the time the US Constitution was adopted in 1787, several states had established churches. Of the fifty-five delegates who attended the Constitutional Convention, an overwhelming majority (fifty of fifty-five) were affiliated with Christian denominations and held orthodox Christian beliefs. Wilson, *Mere Christendom*, 88.

16. Benge and Pickowicz, *American Puritans*, 6–8.

17. The phrase "separation of church and state" is often misunderstood. It was originally meant to ensure that the government would not interfere with religious practices, specifically to prevent the establishment of a national church, such as a "Church of the United States of America." For related information, see Wilson, *Mere Christendom*, 105–12.

18. Benge and Pickowicz, *American Puritans*, 17–19.

Final Remarks

widespread evangelical faith before Christ's visible return to the earth. This does not imply that evil will be entirely absent from the world, but rather that the kingdom of God will advance despite opposition, much like the slow yet unstoppable growth of a mustard seed (Matt 13:31–32).

The introductory chapter defined eschatology and outlined the primary millennial views: amillennialism, premillennialism, dispensationalism, and postmillennialism. Chapter 2 explored hermeneutics, emphasizing the importance of proper interpretation in understanding ancient and biblical texts. Moreover, it discussed the common interpretative approaches to the book of Revelation, such as historicism, idealism, futurism, and preterism.

Chapter 3 examined the optimistic depictions of the Messiah's reign over a vast earthly kingdom as described in the Psalms and the Prophets. This theme was extended into chapter 4, which focused on New Testament passages that affirm the gospel's ultimate triumph and the establishment of Christ's kingdom on the earth, particularly in the Gospel of Matthew, the book of Acts, and the Epistles. Chapter 5 analyzed the Olivet Discourse and its implications for postmillennial eschatology.

Chapter 6 provided a historical and literary analysis of the book of Revelation, covering topics such as authorship, audience relevance, date, genre, structure, and primary theme. Chapter 7 offered a focused exposition of key passages critical for interpreting Revelation and the millennium. Chapter 8 addressed common theological, practical, and biblical objections to postmillennialism, drawing from prominent advocates of the view. Chapter 9 specifically engaged with critiques of postmillennialism by Jeremy Sexton. Finally, chapter 10 discussed the implications of postmillennial thought, including its influence on the founding of the United States of America.

As a final reflection on the eschatological perspective presented in this book, the "millennium" began in the first century with the establishment of Christ's messianic kingdom. Jesus himself indicated that his casting out of demons was a sign of the kingdom of God's arrival (Luke 11:20). This millennium, as described in Rev 20, spans the time between Christ's first and second comings. The kingdom's growth is illustrated by the parable of the mustard seed, where Jesus describes its gradual expansion (Matt 13:31–32). Importantly, this millennium is understood symbolically, representing an indefinite period rather than a literal thousand years (cf. Ps 50:10; 2 Pet 3:8–9).

During this era, the kingdom of God continues to expand as the world is evangelized through the preaching of the gospel and the power of the Holy Spirit, fulfilling the Great Commission (Matt 28:18–20). Christians are called to live righteous lives and contribute to the establishment of just laws that align with God's moral standards (Rom 13:1–5). As the world increasingly turns to Christ, including a significant conversion of ethnic Jews (Rom 11), Satan will be released for a short time to incite rebellion against God's kingdom. Christ will return, defeat Satan, and initiate the final judgment, separating the righteous from the wicked (Rev 20:7–15). Following this, the heavens and earth will undergo a radical transformation, preparing for the eternal reign of God's kingdom (Rev 21:1–5).

Bibliography

Alexander, Joseph A. *Commentary on Psalms*. 1864. Reprint, Grand Rapids: Kregel, 1991.
———. *Isaiah: Translated and Explained*. Vol. 1. New York: Scribner, 1867.
Allis, Oswald T. *Prophecy and the Church*. Philadelphia: P&R, 1945.
Althaus, Paul. *The Theology of Martin Luther*. Philadelphia: Fortress, 1966.
Archer, Gleason L., et al. *Three Views on the Rapture*. Grand Rapids: Zondervan, 1996.
Augustine. *The City of God*. Vol. 6, Books 18.36–20. Translated by William Chase Green. Loeb Classical Library. Cambridge: Harvard University Press, 1960.
Aune, David E. *Revelation 6–16*. Word Biblical Commentary 52B. Grand Rapids: Zondervan, 1998.
———. *Revelation 17–22*. Word Biblical Commentary 52C. Grand Rapids: Zondervan, 1998.
Bahnsen, Greg L. *Victory in Jesus: The Bright Hope of Postmillenialism*. 3rd ed. Nacogdoches, TX: Covenant Media, 2020.
Barton, John. *The Cambridge Companion to Biblical Interpretation*. New York: Cambridge University Press, 1999.
Bass, Clarence B. *Backgrounds to Dispensationalism: Its Historical Genesis and Ecclesiastical Implications*. Grand Rapids: Eerdmans, 1960.
Bauckham, Richard. *Jesus and the Eyewitnesses: The Gospels as Eyewitness Testimony*. 2nd ed. Grand Rapids: Eerdmans, 2017.
Baur, Ferdinand Christian. *The Church History of the First Three Centuries*. 3rd ed. 2 vols. London: Williams & Norgate, 1878–1879.
Beagley, Alan James. *The "Sitz im Leben" of the Apocalypse with Particular Reference to the Role of the Church's Enemies*. New York: Walter de Gruyter, 1987.
Beckwith, Isbon T. *Apocalypse of John: Studies in Introduction with a Critical and Exegetical Commentary*. New York: MacMillan, 1922.
Beeke, Joel R., and Mark Jones. *A Puritan Theology: Doctrine for Life*. Grand Rapids: Reformation Heritage, 2012.
Beeke, Joel R., and Paul M. Smalley. *Reformed Systematic Theology*. Vol 4, *Church and Last Things*. Wheaton, IL: Crossway, 2024.
Benge, Dustin, and Nate Pickowicz. *The American Puritans*. Grand Rapids: Reformation Heritage, 2020.
Berkhof, Louis. *Principles of Biblical Interpretation: Sacred Hermeneutics*. 2nd ed. Grand Rapids: Baker, 1952.
———. *Systematic Theology*. Expanded ed. Edinburgh: Banner of Truth, 2023.

BIBLIOGRAPHY

Beza, Theodore. *The New Testament of Our Lord Jesus Christ*. London: Deputies of Christopher Barker, 1599.

Biguzzi, Giancarlo. "Is the Babylon of Revelation Rome or Jerusalem?" *Biblica* 87:3 (2006) 371–86.

Bloesch, Donald G. *Essentials of Evangelical Theology*. Vol. 2. New York: Harper & Row, 1982.

Blomberg, Craig L., and Sung Wook Chung. *A Case for Historic Premillennialism: An Alternative to "Left Behind" Eschatology*. Grand Rapids: Baker Academic, 2009.

Bock, Darrell L. *Three Views on the Millennium and Beyond*. Grand Rapids: Zondervan, 1999.

Boettner, Loraine. *The Millennium*. Philadelphia: P&R, 1980.

Boring, M. Eugene. *Revelation*. Louisville: John Knox, 1989.

Bray, Gerald. *Biblical Interpretation: Past and Present*. Downers Grove, IL: InterVarsity, 1996.

Brisco, Thomas V. *Holman Bible Atlas: A Complete Guide to the Expansive Geography of Biblical History*. Nashville: B&H, 1998.

Brooks, James A., and Carlton L. Winbery. *Syntax of New Testament Greek*. Washington, DC: University Press of America, 1979.

Brown, Francis, et al. *Brown-Driver-Briggs Hebrew and English Lexicon*. 1906. Reprint, Lancaster, TX: Snowball, 2010.

Brown, Jeannine K. *Scripture as Communication: Introducing Biblical Hermeneutics*. Grand Rapids: Baker Academic, 2007.

Bruce, F. F. *New Testament History*. New York: Doubleday, 1980.

Bultmann, Rudolf. *Essays: Philosophical and Theological*. Translated by James C. G. Greig. London: SCM, 1955.

Callan, Terrance. "Psalm 110:1 and the Origin of the Expectation that Jesus Will Come Again." *Catholic Biblical Quarterly* 44:4 (Oct. 1982) 622–36.

Calvin, John. *Commentaries on the Epistle of Paul the Apostle to the Romans*. Edinburgh: Calvin Translation Society, 1849.

———. *Commentary on the Book of Psalms*. Vol. 1. Translated by James Anderson. Grand Rapids: Eerdmans, 1949.

———. *Commentary on the Book of the Prophet Isaiah*. Vol. 1. Translated by William Pringle. Grand Rapids: Eerdmans, 1953.

———. *Institutes of the Christian Religion*. Translated by Henry Beveridge. Peabody, MA: Hendrickson, 2021.

Campbell, Donald K., and Jeffery L. Townsend. *The Coming Millennial Kingdom: A Case for Premillennial Interpretation*. Grand Rapids: Kregel, 1997.

Cellérier, Jacob Élisée. *Biblical Hermeneutics*. Translated by Charles Elliott and William Justin Harsha. New York: Anson D. F. Randolph, 1881.

Cheyne, T. K. *The Prophecies of Isaiah: A New Translation with Commentary and Appendices*. 5th ed. Vol. 1. New York: Thomas Whittaker, 1895.

Chilton, David. *The Days of Vengeance: An Exposition on the Book of Revelation*. Fort Worth: Dominion, 1990.

———. *Paradise Restored: A Biblical Theology of Dominion*. Tyler, TX: Dominion, 1994.

Clouse, Robert G., ed. *The Meaning of the Millennium: Four Views*. Downers Grove, IL: InterVarsity, 1977.

Collins, Adela Y. "Dating the Apocalypse of John." *Biblical Research* 26 (1981) 33–45.

BIBLIOGRAPHY

Corley, Bruce, et al., eds. *Biblical Hermeneutics: A Comprehensive Introduction to Interpreting Scripture*. 2nd ed. Nashville: B&H, 2002.
Cotton, John. *The Churches Resurrection*. London: Henry Overton, 1642.
Cox, William E. *Amillennialism Today*. Phillipsburg, NJ: P&R, 1966.
Craigie, Peter C., and Marvin E. Tate. *Psalms 1–50*. Word Biblical Commentary 19. 2nd ed. Grand Rapids: Zondervan, 2016.
Cross, F. L., and E. A. Livingstone. *The Oxford Dictionary of the Christian Church*. 2nd ed. New York: Oxford University Press, 1990.
Danker, Frederick W., et al. *Greek-English Lexicon of the New Testament and Other Early Christian Literature*. 3rd ed. Chicago: University of Chicago Press, 2000.
D'Aubigné, J. H. Merle. *The Reformation in England*. 2 vols. 1853. Reprint, Edinburgh: Banner of Truth, 2020.
Davies, P. R. "Daniel Chapter Two." *Journal of Theological Studies* 27:2 (Oct. 1976) 392–401.
Davies, William D. *Paul and Rabbinic Judaism: Some Rabbinic Elements in Pauline Theology*. 2nd ed. London: SPCK, 1955.
Davis, John Jefferson. *Christ's Victorious Kingdom: Postmillennialism Reconsidered*. Grand Rapids: Baker, 1986.
DeMar, Gary, and Francis X. Gumerlock. *New Testament Eschatology: What the Early Church Believed About Bible Prophecy*. Powder Springs, GA: American Vision, 2024.
Dickson, David. *A Commentary on the Psalms*. 1653–55. Reprint, Edinburgh: Banner of Truth, 1995.
Dio Cassius. *Dio's Roman History*. Translated by Earnest Cary. Loeb Classical Library. New York: Macmillan, 1914.
Dockery, David S. *Holman Concise Bible Commentary*. Nashville: B&H, 1998.
Dodd, C. H. "The Fall of Jerusalem and the 'Abomination of Desolation.'" *Journal of Roman Studies* 37 (1947) 47–54.
Doddridge, Philip. *The Family Expositor*. 8th ed. Vol. 6. Charlestown, MA: S. Etheridge, 1808.
Dumbrell, William J. *The Search for Order: Biblical Eschatology in Focus*. Grand Rapids: Baker, 1994.
Edwards, Jonathan. *The Works of Jonathan Edwards*. Vol. 1. 1834. Reprint, Peabody, MA: Hendrickson, 2011.
Ehrman, Bart D., ed. and trans. *The Apostolic Fathers, Volume 1: I Clement, II Clement, Ignatius, Polycarp, Didache*. Loeb Classical Library. Cambridge: Harvard University Press, 2003.
Ellis, Paul. *AD 70 and the End of the World: Finding Good News in Christ's Prophecies and Parables of Judgment*. Birkenhead, New Zealand: KingsPress, 2017.
Elwell, Walter A., ed. *Baker Commentary on the Bible*. Grand Rapids: Baker, 2000.
———. *Evangelical Dictionary of Theology*. 2nd ed. Grand Rapids: Baker Academic, 2001.
Erickson, Millard J. *Christian Theology*. 3rd ed. Grand Rapids: Baker Academic, 2013.
Eusebius. *The Church History*. Translated by Paul L. Maier. Grand Rapids: Kregel, 2007.
Farrar, Frederic W. *History of Interpretation*. London: MacMillan, 1886.
Fee, Gordon D., and Douglas Stuart. *How to Read the Bible for All Its Worth*. 4th ed. Grand Rapids: Zondervan, 2014.
Ferguson, Everett. *Backgrounds of Early Christianity*. 3rd ed. Grand Rapids: Eerdmans, 2003.

Bibliography

Ferguson, Sinclair B., et al. *Church History 101: The Highlights of Twenty Centuries*. Grand Rapids: Reformation Heritage, 2016.
Ford, J. Massyngberde. *Revelation: Introduction, Translation, and Commentary*. Garden City, NY: Doubleday, 1975.
Freehof, Solomon B. *The Book of Psalms*. The Jewish Commentary for Bible Readers. Cincinnati: Union of American Hebrew Congregations, 1938.
Gentry, Kenneth L., Jr. *The Beast of Revelation*. 2nd ed. Fountain Inn, SC: Victorious Hope, 2002.
———. *Before Jerusalem Fell*. Powder Springs, GA: American Vision, 1998.
———. *The Book of Revelation Made Easy: You Can Understand Bible Prophecy*. Powder Springs, GA: American Vision, 2019.
———. *The Divorce of Israel: A Redemptive-Historical Interpretation of Revelation*. 2 vols. Acworth, GA: Tolle Lege, 2024.
———. *The Greatness of the Great Commission: The Christian Enterprise in a Fallen World*. Rev. ed. Tyler, TX: Institute for Christian Economics, 1993.
———. *He Shall Have Dominion: A Postmillennial Eschatology*. 3rd ed. Chesnee, SC: Victorious Hope, 2021.
———. *Navigating the Book of Revelation: Special Studies on Important Issues*. 2nd ed. Fountain Inn, SC: GoodBirth Ministries, 2010.
———. *The Olivet Discourse Made Easy: You Can Understand Jesus' Great Prophetic Discourse*. Chesnee, SC: Victorious Hope, 2021.
———. *Perilous Times: A Study in Eschatological Evil*. Fountain Inn, SC: Victorious Hope, 2012.
———. *Postmillennialism Made Easy*. 2nd ed. Chesnee, SC: Victorious Hope, 2020.
Gerstner, John H. *Wrongly Dividing the Word of Truth: A Critique of Dispensationalism*. Brentwood, TN: Wolgemuth & Hyatt, 1991.
Gill, John. *An Exposition of the Books of the Prophets of the Old Testament*. Vol. 1. London: George Keith, 1757.
———. *An Exposition of the New Testament in Three Volumes*. London: Aaron Ward, 1747.
———. *An Exposition of the Old Testament*. Vol. 3. London: George Keith, 1765.
Goldingay, John. *Psalms, Volume 1: Psalms 1–41*. Edited by Tremper Longman III. Baker Commentary on the Old Testament Wisdom and Psalms. Grand Rapids: Baker Academic, 2006.
Goldsworthy, Graeme. *Gospel-Centered Hermeneutics: Foundations and Principles of Evangelical Biblical Interpretation*. Downers Grove, IL: InterVarsity, 2006.
Gooder, Paula. *Searching for Meaning: An Introduction to Interpreting the New Testament*. Louisville: Westminster John Knox, 2009.
Goodwin, Thomas. *The Works of Thomas Goodwin*. Vol. 12. Edinburgh: James Nichol, 1866.
Grant, Michael. *Herod the Great*. New York: American Heritage, 1971.
Green, Joel B., and Lee Martin McDonald, eds. *The World of the New Testament: Cultural, Social, and Historical Contexts*. Grand Rapids: Baker Academic, 2013.
Gregg, Steve. *Revelation: Four Views; A Parallel Commentary*. Revised and updated. Nashville: Thomas Nelson, 2013.
Grenz, Stanley J. *The Millennial Maze: Sorting Out Evangelical Options*. Downers Grove, IL: InterVarsity, 1992.

BIBLIOGRAPHY

Gribben, Crawford. *An Introduction to John Owen: A Christian Vision for Every Stage of Life.* Wheaton, IL: Crossway, 2020.

Grudem, Wayne. *Politics According to the Bible: A Comprehensive Resource for Understanding Modern Political Issues in Light of Scripture.* Grand Rapids: Zondervan, 2010.

―――. *Systematic Theology: An Introduction to Biblical Doctrine.* 2nd ed. Grand Rapids: Zondervan, 2020.

Gumerlock, Francis X. "Nero Antichrist: Patristic Evidence for the Use of Nero's Naming in Calculating the Number of the Beast (Rev 13:18)." *Westminster Theological Journal* 68:2 (Fall 2006) 347–60.

Gundry, Robert H. *Commentary on the New Testament: Verse-by-Verse Explanations with a Literal Translation.* Vol. 2. Grand Rapids: Baker Academic, 2010.

Guthrie, Donald. *New Testament Introduction.* 4th ed. Downers Grove, IL: InterVarsity, 1990.

Guyse, John. *The Practical Expositor.* 5th ed. Vol. 6. Edinburgh: Ross & Sons, 1797.

Hagner, Donald A. *Matthew 1–13.* Word Biblical Commentary 33a. Grand Rapids: Zondervan, 2014.

Hamilton, Floyd E. *The Basis of Millennial Faith.* Grand Rapids: Eerdmans, 1952.

Harrison, R. K. *Jeremiah and Lamentations: An Introduction and Commentary.* Downers Grove, IL: InterVarsity, 1973.

Hartley, David. *Observations on Man: His Frame, His Duty, and His Expectations.* 4th ed. Vol. 2. London: J. Johnson, 1801.

Hay, David M. *Glory at the Right Hand: Psalm 110 in Early Christianity.* Nashville: Abingdon, 1973.

Hemer, Colin J. *Letters to the Seven Churches of Asia in Their Local Setting.* Sheffield, UK: Sheffield Academic, 1989.

Hendriksen, William. *More Than Conquerors: An Interpretation of the Book of Revelation.* 1939. Reprint, Grand Rapids: Baker Book House, 1971.

Hennecke, Edgar, et al., eds. *New Testament Apocrypha.* Vol. 2. Philadelphia: Westminster, 1965.

Henry, Matthew. *Matthew Henry's Commentary on the Whole Bible.* 6 vols. McLean, VA: MacDonald, 1970.

Herbert, A. S. *Isaiah 1–39.* The Cambridge Bible Commentary. Cambridge: Cambridge University Press, 1973.

Hernando, James D. *Dictionary of Hermeneutics: A Concise Guide to Terms, Names, Methods, and Expressions.* Springfield, MO: Gospel, 2012.

Hiebert, D. Edmond. *1 and 2 Thessalonians.* Winona Lake, IN: BMH Books, 2007.

Hill, Andrew E. *Haggai, Zechariah and Malachi: An Introduction and Commentary.* Downers Grove, IL: InterVarsity, 2012.

Hill, Charles E. *Regnum Caelorum: Patterns of Millennial Thought in Early Christianity.* 2nd ed. Grand Rapids: Eerdmans, 2001.

Hill, David. *The Gospel of Matthew.* The New Century Bible Commentary. Grand Rapids: Eerdmans, 1981.

Hillegonds, Robert. *The Early Date of Revelation and the End Times.* Fountain Inn, SC: Victorious Hope, 2016.

Hitchcock, Mark L. "A Defense of the Domitianic Date of the Book of Revelation." PhD diss., Dallas Theological Seminary, 2005.

Hodge, Charles. *Commentary on the Epistle to the Romans.* 1886. Reprint, Grand Rapids: Eerdmans, 1960.

Holwerda, David E. *Exploring the Heritage of John Calvin*. Grand Rapids: Baker Book House, 1976.
Hopkins, Samuel. *A Treatise on the Millennium*. Religion in America. 1793. Reprint, New York: Arno, 1972.
House, H. Wayne, and Thomas D. Ice. *Dominion Theology: Blessing or Curse?* Portland, OR: Multnomah, 1988.
Ice, Thomas, and Kenneth L. Gentry Jr. *The Great Tribulation, Past or Future?* Grand Rapids: Kregel, 1999.
Jamieson, Robert, et al. *A Commentary on the Old and New Testaments*. 3 vols. 1871. Reprint, Peabody, MA: Hendrickson, 2002.
Josephus, Flavius. *The Antiquities of the Jews*. Translated by William Whiston. Scotts Valley, CA: Createspace Independent Publishing Platform, 2016.
———. *The Jewish War*. Translated by G. A. Williamson. New York: Penguin, 1981.
Kaiser, Otto. *Isaiah 1–12: A Commentary*. Philadelphia: Westminster, 1972.
Kaiser, Walter C., Jr., and Moisés Silva. *Introduction to Biblical Hermeneutics: The Search for Meaning*. Grand Rapids: Zondervan, 2007.
Keener, Craig S. *The IVP Bible Background Commentary: New Testament*. 2nd ed. Downers Grove, IL: InterVarsity, 2014.
Kidner, Derek. *Psalms 73–150*. Kidner Classic Commentaries. Downers Grove, IL: InterVarsity, 2008.
Kik, J. Marcellus. *The Eschatology of Victory*. Philadelphia: P&R, 1971.
King, Max R. *The Cross and the Parousia of Christ: The Two Dimensions of One Age-Changing Eschaton*. Warren, OH: Parkman Road Church of Christ, 1987.
Klein, William W., et al. *Introduction to Biblical Interpretation*. 3rd ed. Grand Rapids: Zondervan, 2017.
Koester, Craig R. "The Number of the Beast in Revelation 13 in Light of Papyri, Graffiti, and Inscriptions." *Journal of Early Christian History* 6:3 (2016) 1–21.
———. *Revelation: A New Translation with Introduction and Commentary*. New Haven: Yale University Press, 2014.
Ladd, George Eldon. *The Gospel of the Kingdom: Scriptural Studies in the Kingdom of God*. Grand Rapids: Eerdmans, 1959.
LaHaye, Tim. *Revelation: Illustrated and Made Plain*. Grand Rapids: Zondervan, 1975.
LaHaye, Tim, and Thomas Ice. *The End Times Controversy*. Eugene, OR: Harvest, 2003.
Law, David R. *The Historical-Critical Method: A Guide for the Perplexed*. New York: T&T Clark, 2012.
Lee, Francis Nigel. *John's Revelation Unveiled*. Brisbane, AU: Queensland Presbyterian Theological College, 2000.
Levine, Lee I. *Judaism and Hellenism in Antiquity: Conflict or Confluence?* Seattle: University of Washington Press, 1998.
Lightner, Robert. *Last Days Handbook*. Nashville: Thomas Nelson, 1997.
Lindsey, Hal, and C. C. Carlson. *The Late Great Planet Earth*. Grand Rapids: Zondervan, 1970.
Luther, Martin. "Twenty-Fifth Sunday after Trinity." In *Sermons of Martin Luther*. Translated by John Nicholas Lenker et al., 5:363–78. 1905. Reprint, Grand Rapids: Baker, 1989.
MacArthur, John. *1 and 2 Thessalonians*. The MacArthur New Testament Commentary. Chicago: Moody, 2002.

BIBLIOGRAPHY

———. *Essential Christian Doctrine: A Handbook on Biblical Truth.* Wheaton, IL: Crossway, 2021.

———. *The MacArthur Bible Commentary.* Nashville: Thomas Nelson, 2005.

———. *Matthew 24–28.* The MacArthur New Testament Commentary. Chicago: Moody, 1989.

MacCulloch, Diarmaid. *All Things Made New: The Reformation and Its Legacy.* New York: Oxford University Press, 2016.

———. *The Reformation: A History.* New York: Viking Penguin, 2004.

MacDonald, William. *Believer's Bible Commentary.* 2nd ed. Nashville: Thomas Nelson, 2016.

Mathison, Keith A. *From Age to Age: The Unfolding of Biblical Eschatology.* Phillipsburg, NJ: P&R, 2014.

———. *Postmillennialism: An Eschatology of Hope.* Phillipsburg, NJ: P&R, 1999.

———. *When Shall These Things Be? A Reformed Response to Hyper-Preterism.* Phillipsburg, NJ: P&R, 2004.

Maurice, Frederick Denison. *Lectures on the Apocalypse.* 1861. Reprint, Frankfurt: Salzwasser Verlag, 2022.

Mazzaferri, Frederick David. *The Genre of the Book of Revelation from a Source-Critical Perspective.* Berlin: Walter de Gruyter, 1989.

McCartney, Dan, and Charles Clayton. *Let the Reader Understand: A Guide to Interpreting and Applying the Bible.* Wheaton, IL: Victor, 1994.

McIver, Robert K. "The Parable of the Weeds Among the Wheat (Matt 13:24–30, 36–43) and the Relationship Between the Kingdom and the Church as Portrayed in the Gospel of Matthew." *Journal of Biblical Literature* 114:4 (Winter 1995) 643–59.

McKim, Donald K. *Westminster Dictionary of Theological Terms.* Louisville: Westminster John Knox, 1996.

McLaren, James S. "Jews and the Imperial Cult: From Augustus to Domitian." *Journal for the Study of the New Testament* 27:3 (Mar. 2005) 257–78.

Meadowcroft, Tim. "Metaphor, Narrative, Interpretation, and Reader in Daniel 2–5." *Narrative* 8:3 (Oct. 2000) 257–78.

Meeter, John E., ed. *Selected Shorter Writings of Benjamin B. Warfield.* Vol. 1. Nutley, NJ: P&R, 1970.

Metzger, Bruce M. *A Textual Commentary on the Greek New Testament.* Corrected ed. Stuttgart: United Bible Societies, 1975.

Minear, Paul S. *I Saw a New Earth: An Introduction to the Visions of the Apocalypse.* Washington, DC: Corpus, 1968.

Moore, Thomas Verner. *A Commentary on Zechariah.* London: Banner of Truth, 1958.

Moorhead, James H. "The Erosion of Postmillennialism in American Religious Thought, 1865–1925." *Church History* 53:1 (Mar. 1984) 61–77.

Morris, Leon. *The Revelation of St. John: An Introduction and Commentary.* Downers Grove, IL: InterVarsity, 1977.

Motyer, J. Alec. *Isaiah: An Introduction and Commentary.* Downers Grove, IL: InterVarsity, 1999.

Mounce, Robert H. *The New International Commentary on the New Testament: The Book of Revelation.* Rev. ed. Grand Rapids: Eerdmans, 1997.

Muilenburg, James. "Form Criticism and Beyond." *Journal of Biblical Literature* 88:1 (Mar. 1969) 1–18.

BIBLIOGRAPHY

Murray, George L. *Millennial Studies: A Search for Truth*. Grand Rapids: Baker House Books, 1960.

Murray, Iain H. *The Puritan Hope: Revival and the Interpretation of Prophecy*. 1971. Reprint, Edinburgh: Banner of Truth, 2021.

Murray, John. *The Epistle to the Romans: The English Text with Introduction, Exposition and Notes*. Vol. 2. Grand Rapids: Eerdmans, 1965.

Newsom, Carol A. *Daniel: A Commentary*. Louisville: Westminster John Knox, 2014.

Nicholson, E. W. *Jeremiah 26–52*. The Cambridge Bible Commentary. Cambridge: Cambridge University Press, 1975.

Nicoll, W. Robertson, ed. *The Expositor's Greek Testament*. 5 vols. Peabody, MA: Hendrickson, 2002.

North, Gary. *Dominion and Common Grace: The Biblical Basis of Progress*. Tyler, TX: Institute for Christian Economics, 1987.

Oliver, Robert W., ed. *John Owen: The Man and His Theology*. Phillipsburg, NJ: P&R, 2002.

Origen. *Contra Celsum*. Translated by Henry Chadwick. Cambridge: Cambridge University Press, 1953.

Osborne, Grant R. *The Hermeneutical Spiral: A Comprehensive Introduction to Biblical Interpretation*. Downers Grove, IL: InterVarsity, 1991.

———. *Revelation*. Baker Exegetical Commentary on the New Testament. Grand Rapids: Baker Academic, 2002.

Pate, C. Marvin. *Interpreting Revelation and Other Apocalyptic Literature: An Exegetical Handbook*. Edited by John D. Harvey. Grand Rapids: Kregel, 2016.

Patterson, Paige. *Revelation: An Exegetical and Theological Exposition of Holy Scripture*. Nashville: B&H, 2012.

Paul, Ian. *Revelation: An Introduction and Commentary*. Downers Grove, IL: InterVarsity, 2018.

Pentecost, J. Dwight. *Thy Kingdom Come: Tracing God's Kingdom Program and Covenant Promises Throughout History*. Grand Rapids: Kregel, 1995.

Petersen, David L. *Zechariah 9–14 and Malachi: A Commentary*. Louisville: Westminster John Knox, 1995.

Pfeiffer, Charles F. *Baker's Bible Atlas*. Grand Rapids: Baker, 1964.

Philo. *Philo in Ten Volumes*. Vol. 8. Translated by F. H. Colson. Loeb Classical Library. Cambridge: Harvard University Press, 1968.

Pliny the Elder. *Natural History*. Vol. 5, *Books 17–19*. Translated by H. Rackham. Loeb Classical Library. Cambridge: Harvard University Press, 1964.

Poole, Matthew. *A Commentary on the Holy Bible*. 3 vols. 1685. Reprint, Peabody, MA: Hendrickson, 1985.

Porteous, Norman W. *Daniel: A Commentary*. Philadelphia: Westminster, 1965.

Potter, H. D. "The New Covenant in Jeremiah XXXI 31–34." *Vetus Testamentum* 33:3 (July 1983) 347–57.

Purkiser, W. T. "Psalms." In *Job Through Song of Solomon*, edited by A. F. Harper et al., 126–452. Beacon Bible Commentary 3. Kansas City, MO: Beacon Hill, 1967.

Quandt, Jean B. "Religion and Social Thought: The Secularization of Postmillennialism." *American Quarterly* 25:4 (Oct. 1973) 390–409.

Quintern, Jason L. "Babylon Unveiled: A Pre-A. D. 70 Interpretation of Revelation's Harlot." *Ecclesia Militans Journal* 2 (forthcoming 2025).

———. "A Defense of the Neronic Date of the Book of Revelation." PhD diss., Liberty University, 2024.

BIBLIOGRAPHY

Ramm, Bernard L. *Protestant Biblical Interpretation: A Textbook of Hermeneutics*. 3rd ed. Grand Rapids: Baker, 1978.

Ramsay, W. M. *The Letters to the Seven Churches of Asia: And Their Place in the Plan of the Apocalypse*. London: Hodder & Stoughton, 1904.

Ratton, James J. L. *The Apocalypse of St. John: A Commentary on the Greek Text*. 2nd ed. London: R. & T. Washbourne, 1915.

Resseguie, James L. *The Revelation of John: A Narrative Commentary*. Grand Rapids: Baker Academic, 2009.

Reynolds, Benjamin E. *John Among the Apocalypses: Jewish Apocalyptic Tradition and the "Apocalyptic" Gospel*. Oxford: Oxford University Press, 2020.

Ridderbos, Herman. *The Coming of the Kingdom*. Philadelphia: P&R, 1962.

Riddlebarger, Kim. *A Case for Amillennialism: Understanding the End Times*. Grand Rapids: Baker, 2013.

Robinson, John A. T. *Redating the New Testament*. Eugene, OR: Wipf & Stock, 2000.

Rogers, Jay. *In the Days of These Kings: The Book of Daniel in Preterist Perspective*. Clermont, FL: Media House International, 2017.

———. *The Prophecy of Daniel in Preterist Perspective: The Easy Parts and the Hard Parts*. Clermont, FL: Media House International, 2021.

Rosenstein, Marc J. *Turning Points in Jewish History*. Philadelphia: Jewish Publication Society, 2018.

Rowland, Christopher. *The Open Heaven: A Study of Apocalyptic in Judaism and Early Christianity*. New York: Crossroad, 1982.

Rushdoony, R. J. *God's Plan for Victory: The Meaning of Postmillennialism*. 3rd ed. Vallecito, CA: Chalcedon Foundation, 2022.

———. "Postmillennialism Versus Impotent Religion." *Journal of Christian Reconstruction* 3:2 (Winter 1976–77) 122–27.

Russell, James Stuart. *The Parousia: A Critical Inquiry Into the New Testament Doctrine of Our Lord's Second Coming*. London: Daldy, Isbister, 1878.

Ryrie, Charles Caldwell. *The Basis of the Premillennial Faith*. Neptune, NJ: Loizeaux Brothers, 1989.

———. *Dispensationalism Today*. Chicago: Moody, 1965.

Sandlin, P. Andrew. *A Postmillennial Primer: Basics of Optimistic Eschatology*. Vallecito, CA: Chalcedon Foundation, 1997. Self-published reprint, 2023.

Schlatter, Adolf. *The Theology of the Apostles: The Development of New Testament Theology*. Translated by Andreas J. Köstenberger. Grand Rapids: Baker, 1999.

Schökel, Luis Alonso. *A Manual of Hermeneutics*. Sheffield, UK: Sheffield Academic, 1998.

Schweitzer, Albert. *The Quest of the Historical Jesus: A Critical Study of Its Progress from Reimarus to Wrede*. 2nd ed. Translated by W. Montgomery. London: Adam & Charles Black, 1911.

Scott, Thomas. *The Holy Bible Containing the Old and New Testaments*. Vol. 3. Philadelphia: J. B. Lippincott, 1866.

Sexton, Jeremy. "Postmillennialism: A Biblical Critique." *Themelios* 48:3 (2023) 551–72.

Shelley, Bruce L., and Marshall Shelley. *Church History in Plain Language*. 5th ed. Grand Rapids: Zondervan, 2021.

Showers, Renald. *Maranatha: Our Lord, Come!* Bellmawr, NJ: Friends of Israel Gospel Ministry, 1995.

Smalley, Stephen S. *The Revelation to John: A Commentary on the Greek Text of the Apocalypse*. Downers Grove, IL: InterVarsity, 2005.

———. *Thunder and Love: John's Revelation and John's Community*. 1994. Reprint, Eugene, OR: Wipf & Stock, 2012.
Sproul, R. C. *Acts: An Expositional Commentary*. Sanford, FL: Ligonier Ministries, 2019.
———. *The Last Days According to Jesus*. Grand Rapids: Baker, 1998.
———. *Matthew: An Expositional Commentary*. Sanford, FL: Ligonier Ministries, 2019.
———. *Romans: An Expositional Commentary*. Sanford, FL: Ligonier Ministries, 2019.
Stein, Stephen J. "The Quest for the Spiritual Sense: The Biblical Hermeneutics of Jonathan Edwards." *Harvard Theological Review* 70:1 (1977) 99–113.
Storms, Sam. *Kingdom Come: The Amillennial Alternative*. Fearn, Scotland: Mentor Imprint, 2020.
Strabo. *The Geography of Strabo*. Vol. 6. Translated by Horace Leonard Jones. Loeb Classical Library. Cambridge: Harvard University Press, 1960.
Stuart, Moses. *A Commentary on the Apocalypse*. 2 vols. Andover, MA: Allen, Morrill & Wardwell, 1845.
Suetonius. *The Twelve Caesars*. Translated by Robert Graves. New York: Penguin, 2003.
Swaggart, Jimmy. *Armageddon: The Future of Planet Earth*. Baton Rouge: Jimmy Swaggart Ministries, 1987.
Sweetnam, Mark, and Crawford Gribben. "J. N. Darby and the Irish Origins of Dispensationalism." *Journal of Evangelical Theological Society* 52:3 (Sept. 2009) 569–77.
Swete, Henry B. *The Apocalypse of St. John: The Greek Text with Introduction Notes and Indices*. 3rd ed. London: MacMillan, 1911.
Swim, Roy E. "Daniel." In *Isaiah Through Daniel*, edited by A. F. Harper et al., 618–88. Beacon Bible Commentary 4. Kansas City, MO: Beacon Hill, 1966.
Tacitus. *Annals*. Translated by Cynthia Damon. New York: Penguin, 2012.
———. *The Histories*. Translated by Kenneth Wellesley. New York: Penguin, 2009.
Taylor, John B. *Ezekiel: An Introduction and Commentary*. Downers Grove, IL: InterVarsity, 1969.
Terry, Milton S. *The Apocalypse of John: A Preterist Commentary on the Book of Revelation*. Chesnee, SC: Victorious Hope, 2021.
———. *Biblical Hermeneutics: A Treatise on the Interpretation of the Old and New Testaments*. New York: Phillips & Hunt, 1885.
Thomas, John C., and Frank D. Macchia. *The Two Horizons New Testament Commentary: Revelation*. Grand Rapids: Eerdmans, 2016.
Thomas, Robert L. *Revelation 1–7: An Exegetical Commentary*. Chicago: Moody, 1992.
Thompson, Leonard L. *The Book of Revelation: Apocalypse and Empire*. New York: Oxford University Press, 1997.
Touilleux, Paul. *L'Apocalypse et les Cultes de Domitien et de Cybele*. Paris: Librairie Orientaliste Paul Geuthner, 1935.
Venema, Cornelis P. *The Promise of the Future*. Edinburgh: Banner of Truth, 2009.
Vielhauer, Philipp. "Introduction to Apocalypses and Related Subjects." In *New Testament Apocrypha*, edited by Edgar Hennecke et al., 2:581–608. Philadelphia: Westminster, 1965.
Virkler, Henry A. *Hermeneutics: Principles and Processes of Biblical Interpretation*. Grand Rapids: Baker, 1995.
Visser, A. J. "A Bird's Eye View of Ancient Christian Eschatology." *Numen* 14:1 (Mar. 1967) 4–22.

BIBLIOGRAPHY

Vorster, W. S. "'Genre' and the Revelation of John: A Study in Text, Context, and Intertext." *Neotestamentica* 22:1 (1988) 103–23.
Vos, Geerhardus. *The Eschatology of the Old Testament*. Edited by James T. Dennison Jr. Phillipsburg, NJ: P&R, 2001.
Wainwright, Arthur W. *Mysterious Apocalypse: Interpreting the Book of Revelation*. 1993. Reprint, Eugene, OR: Wipf & Stock, 2001.
Walton, John H., et al. *The IVP Bible Background Commentary: Old Testament*. Downers Grove, IL: InterVarsity, 2000.
Walvoord, John F. *Every Prophecy of the Bible*. Colorado Springs: Chariot Victor, 1999.
———. *The Millennial Kingdom*. Findlay, OH: Dunham, 1963.
———. *The Revelation of Jesus Christ*. Chicago: Moody, 1972.
Warfield, Benjamin B. *Biblical and Theological Studies*. Philadelphia: P&R, 1952.
Watts, John D. W. *Isaiah 1–33*. Word Biblical Commentary 24. Grand Rapids: Zondervan, 2004.
Weber, Joseph C. "Karl Barth and the Historical Jesus." *Journal of Bible and Religion* 32:4 (Oct. 1964) 350–54.
Whitby, Daniel. "A Treatise of the True Millennium." In *A Paraphrase and Commentary on the New Testament*, 2:251–78. London: Black Swan, 1703.
White, James R. *Scripture Alone: Exploring the Bible's Accuracy, Authority, and Authenticity*. Minneapolis,: Bethany House, 2004.
Wilson, Douglas. *Heaven Misplaced: Christ's Kingdom on Earth*. Moscow, ID: Canon, 2008.
———. *Mere Christendom*. Moscow, ID: Canon, 2023.
———. *When the Man Comes Around: A Commentary on the Book of Revelation*. Moscow, ID: Canon, 2019.
Wolfe, Stephen. *The Case for Christian Nationalism*. Moscow, ID: Canon, 2022.
Yarchin, William. *History of Biblical Interpretation: A Reader*. Peabody, MA: Hendrickson, 2004.
Youngblood, Ronald F. *Nelson's Illustrated Bible Dictionary: New and Enhanced Edition*. Nashville: Thomas Nelson, 2014.
Zakai, Avihu. *Exile and Kingdom: History and Apocalypse in the Puritan Migration to America*. Cambridge: Cambridge University Press, 1992.

Scripture Index

OLD TESTAMENT

Genesis

1:26–28	44
2:15–17	44
12:3	39, 60
14:18–20	37
18:8	39
22:18	39
48:14–20	36

Exodus

15	31
15:6	36
23:29	65

Leviticus

4:32–33	135
23:10	65
23:10–11	61

Numbers

15:19–21	61
20:18–21	85n43
21:14	22

Deuteronomy

9:5	137
29:4	64
32:21	70n16

1 Samuel

10:1	33
16:1–3	41

2 Samuel

2:8	30
5:6	30
5:17	30
7:11–16	40
7:14	32
7:18	41
23:1–5	40

1 Kings

8:25	40
8:41–43	103
12:1–20	40
17:17–24	65
19:18	33

2 Kings

4:32–37	65
15:29	40
19:21	31
22:1	45

1 Chronicles

14:8	30

Scripture Index

2 Chronicles

4:9	103
36:11–21	45

Psalms

	29
2	29, 30, 31, 34, 51
2:1	30, 104
2:1–3	29
2:1–6	34
2:3	30
2:4–6	31
2:5	31
2:6	31, 34, 37
2:7	32
2:7–8	34
2:7–9	32
2:8	32
2:9	32
2:9–12	34
2:10–12	33
2:11	33
2:12	33
2:27–28	35
16	59
18:7–15	74, 97, 102, 135
19:4	70
20:7	34
22	34, 35, 51
22:1–2	34
37:13	31
44:6	34
46:4	47
48:1–2	31
50:10	109, 143
59:8	31
62:6–8	34
65:9	47
69:22–23	64
96:10	35
97:1	35
99:1	35
104:3	74, 97, 102, 135
110	34, 35, 36, 51, 58n20, 59
110:1	8, 37, 58, 58n20, 65n41
110:1–4	36
110:2	37
110:3	37
110:4	37
115:3	120, 138
118:8	34
137:7	85n43
146:3	34

Proverbs

1:26–27	31

Isaiah

1:21	108
2	37
2:1–4	38, 38n34
2:2	38
2:2–4	31
6:9–10	64
7:14	40
9	39
9:6–7	40, 65n41
11	41
11:1	41
11:2	41
11:9–12	41
11:10	42
11:11–12	42
11:20	42n60
11:21	42n60
11:22	42n60
11:25	64n38
11:26	64, 64n38
13:10	74
13–23	137
17:12	104
19:1	74, 97, 102, 135
19:23–25	46
24:23	38
29:10	64
32:15	38
33:20–24	47
34:4	74
37:32	38
40:22–23	31
41:10	36
42:6	59

42:13	41n52	34:23	40
46:10	119	34:24	40
49:6	32, 57n15, 59	37:24	40
53:1	37	38	112, 133
53:5–6	34	39	112, 133
55:11	119	40:3	102
56:7	103	40:17	103
57:20	104	47	46
60:3	57n15	47:1–9	47, 54, 133
60:5	104		
65	43		

Daniel

65:17	42, 43
65:17–25	42, 43
65:20	43, 44	2	49, 71
65:21	44	2	47, 49
65:22	44	2:31–35	48, 54, 133
65:23	43, 44	2:34–35	33n15
		2:35	50
		2:44	33n15, 48, 54, 133
		7	49, 104

Jeremiah

		7:2–3	104
1:1–3	45	7:13	97
2:2	108	7:13–14	49, 65n41
2:20	108	8:13	71
3:1	108	11:31	71, 72n19
3:2	108		
3:6	108		

Hosea

3:8	108	1:2	108
3:16–17	46	3:5	40
4:30	108	13:2	33
5:20–25	45		
5:25	45		

Joel

6:22–23	104		
11:15	108	2:1	97
13:27	108	2:1–2	74, 102, 135
30:9	40	2:2	97
31	44, 45	2:10	74
31:31–34	45	2:31	74
48:7	46	2:32	38
49:6	46		
49:39	46		

Amos

51:42	104	8:9	74

Ezekiel

Obadiah

16	108		
25–32	137	1:17	38
26:3	104	1:21	38
32:7	74		

Scripture Index

21

Micah

4:1–3
4:7
5:2–4
6:7

Nahum

1

35

38, 38n34
38
40
109

97, 102

Zephaniah

1:14   97
1:14–15   102
1:15   97

Zechariah

9   50
9:9–10   50
12:10   38, 63, 97, 102, 135
14:9   35

ANCIENT NEAR EASTERN TEXTS

Narmer Palette

32n14

DEUTEROCANONICAL BOOKS

1 Enoch

10:4–6   111, 111n47

88:1   111

ANCIENT JEWISH WRITERS

Josephus

81, 86, 107, 135

Antiquities

4.15.2   85n43
5.2.10   135n26
6.6.3   135n26
18:2:2   82n27
18.8.2   86n44
19.8.2   86n45
20.2   68n3

Jewish War

2.13   68n3
5–6   126n45

5.5.4   107n32

Philo

135

Special Laws

4.36 § 192   135n27

Scripture Index

NEW TESTAMENT

Matthew

	52–57, 53n1, 66, 143
3:2	53
3:17	32
4:5	72
4:17	48, 53, 53n1
5:3–12	120
5–7	120
6:9–13	52
6:10	53, 137, 138
7:13–14	120, 120n22, 122, 128
7:15–20	55, 120
7:24–27	120
10:5–6	57n15
11:16	75
12:14	108
12:27–29	48
12:29	113
12:39	75
12:41–42	75
12:45	75
13:22	118
13:24	123
13:24–30	54, 130, 132
13:31–32	54, 118, 130, 143
13:31–33	53n1, 133
13:33	55
13:36–39	122, 128
13:36–43	54, 132
13:38	123, 133
13:39	123
13:47–49	133
13:47–50	54
14:4	137
16:13–16	49
16:18	49
17:5	32
17:17	75
19:23–24	53n1
20:18–19	97, 102, 135
21:1–11	50
21:44	33
22:15–22	88
22:44	36
22:46	36
23:34–37	107
23:37	108n34
23:38—24:3	72
24	67, 67n1, 72, 74, 76
24:1–2	67, 68
24:1–3	74
24:3	102
24:3–13	68
24:14	68, 69, 70, 76
24:15	71, 72, 75
24:15–22	71
24:15–35	73
24:16	72
24:17–20	73
24:22	71n18
24:24	111n46
24:29–30	73
24:30	49, 74
24:32–35	74
24:34	74, 75
24:42	119
25:13	119
25:31–46	54
26:3–4	108
26:59	108, 135
26:64	36, 49, 102
26:66	135
27:1	108, 135
27:2	135n23
27:11	135n23
27:11–25	97, 102
27:11–26	107
27:27	135n23
27:46	34
27:53	72
28:18	56, 130, 138
28:18–20	2, 55, 59, 113, 129–30, 136, 144
28:19	56, 137
28:19–20	39
28:20	137
28:30	130

Mark

	52

Scripture Index

1:14	69n12
1:15	53n1
4:30–32	53n1
10:33	97, 102
12:36	36
13	67, 75
14:62	36
15:1	97, 102
16:19	36

Luke

	52
1:1	22
2:1	68
2:36	97
8:4–15	93
11:20	143
15:11–32	93
18:1	124
18:7–8	123–24, 128
18:8	123, 124n38
18:32	30, 97, 102
19:27	33
20:41–44	36
21	67, 75
21:20	75
21:24	103
21:29	75
22:20	46
22:36	137
22:69	36
23:1–2	97, 102

John

	47, 52, 67n2, 79, 79n15
2:19–21	47
3:3	63n34
3:5	63n34
4:14	47
5:24–25	8
6:37	32
7:38	47
8:44	110
10:12	32
11:1–44	65
11:25–26	8
12:33	100
18:28–31	97, 102
18:32	100
19:12–15	97, 102
19:30	116
19:34	47

Acts

	52, 58, 66, 69n10, 143
1:9	50
1:11	74, 102, 120
2	70
2:5	70
2:10	70n14
2:16–17	38
2:16–21	38
2:22–23	97
2:24	34
2:29–35	40
2:30–36	58
2:32–36	8
2:33	36, 47
2:33–35	36
2:34–35	37
3:13	97, 102
3:13–15	97
4:25	30
4:25–26	30
4:25–27	30
4:26–27	97, 102
4:27	30
4:33	70n12
5:28–30	97
7:52	97, 108
9:17	63n34
10:39	97
10:45	69
11:18	69
11:28	68n7
12	86
12:20–23	86
13	59
13:1	77n3
13:13–43	59
13:14	59
13:21	97
13:32–33	30

13:44–47	59	11:11–12	60, 60n24, 62
13:46–47	59	11:11–26	60, 63
21:21	69	11:11–32	64n38
24:5	68n7, 69	11:12	61
24–25	86	11:12–25	42
24:25	137	11:13–15	60
26:1–2	86	11:16–21	61
		11:22–24	62
		11:23–25	62

Romans

	66	11:25	63, 120
1:3–4	36	11:25–26	63
1:4	56	13:1	138
1:5	69	13:1–5	144
1:16	37, 57n15, 116	16:20	101
2:28–29	62	20:7–15	144
3:23–26	34	21:1–5	144
3:29–30	35		
5:20	116		

1 Corinthians

6:4–5	112	1:10	63n34
6:9	65	3:16	42
6:12	117	11–13	77n3
6:16	30	12:28	77n3
7:21–23	118	15	65n41, 66
7:24	118	15:20	112
8:2	117	15:20–28	64–65
8:11	117	15:22–24	8
8:17	117	15:24–26	134
8:18–25	114	15:24–28	34, 65, 129, 131–32, 136
8:20	117	15:25	36, 50
8:22	117	15:53–57	117
8:28	117		
8:29–30	138		

2 Corinthians

8:34	36	3:4–6	46
9:6–9	62	4:17	117
9:6–29	60n24	5:17	42, 43
9:22–23	33	5:21	34
9:22–30	62	10:3–4	110
9:30—10:4	60n24		
9:30–33	60n24		

Galatians

10:12	32		
10:14	138	3:13	34
10:18	70	3:23–29	62
10:19	70n16	3:28	57n15
11	120, 144	6:15	43
11:1	61, 97	6:15–16	62
11:5	63		
11:7–10	63		

Ephesians

1:4–5	138
1:11	119
1:20	36
1:20–22	8
2:1–6	8
2:4–5	116
2:13–14	32
2:22	42
6:12	110

Philippians

1:6	116
2:8–9	56
3:5	97

Colossians

	68n5
1:5–6	68
1:6	70
1:18	112
1:23	70
1:27	42
3:1	36
3:1–4	8

1 Thessalonians

	125, 125n40, 126
2:13	78
2:14–15	97
4:13–18	125
4:15–17	7n25, 74, 102
5:1–6	125

2 Thessalonians

	125, 125n40, 126
1:8	113
1:8–9	33
2:1–3	125
2:1–4	124–26, 128
2:4	125
2:6	125

1 Timothy

2:1–4	137
2:5	36
5:1–2	63n34

2 Timothy

3	126, 127
3:1–4	126–27, 128
3:10	126
3:13	126–27, 128
3:16	78

Hebrews

1:2	3, 38
1:3	36
1:5	30
1:13	36
5:5	32
5:6	36
7:3	37
7:14	97
7:17	36
7:21	36
7:22	46
8:6–13	46
9:4	103
9:15	46
9:26	38
10:12	36
10:12–13	36
10:14–18	46
10:29	46
12:2	36
12:18	37
12:18–17	38
12:22	31
12:22–24	46
12:24	37
13:1	63n34

1 Peter

1:20	3, 38
2:14	137
2:24	34

SCRIPTURE INDEX

5:8	110	11:1–2	102–3
		11:2	103
		11:3	103
		11:8	107, 108

2 Peter

3:8–9	143
3:13	44

11:14	101
12:6	103
12:7–9	110
12:7–17	110
12:14	103

1 John

2:18	3
2:26	111n46

13	87
13:1	80, 104
13:1–4	103–5
13:3	105
13:4–15	84

Revelation

5, 11, 15, 23, 24, 24n46, 25, 25n51, 28, 52, 67n2, 74, 74n27, 77, 78, 79, 79n11, 79n15, 80, 82, 83, 84, 84n42, 85, 86, 87, 88, 91, 93, 94n80, 95, 96, 97, 98, 99, 100, 101, 101n7, 103, 109, 113, 114, 129, 136, 143

1:1	77, 83, 94, 100, 101, 120
1:1–5	100
1:1–9	99–102
1:3	83, 100, 101, 120
1:4	77
1:7	74, 96, 96n94, 97, 98, 101, 102, 135
1:9	77, 84, 88, 101, 112
1:10–11	83, 101
1:19	83
2:1–7	89
2–3	89, 98
2:9	90, 112
2:13	90
2:16	101
2:26	112
3:4	91
3:9–10	112
3:11	101
3:12	92
3:17–18	92
3:21	112
4:4	111
4–5	95
5:9	98
5:11	109
6:9	111
8:11	121

13:5	85, 103
13:5–10	84
13:11	135
13:12	104
13:14	110
13:18	80, 82
14:9–11	84
16:2	84
16:13	135
16:19	107, 108
17:1–6	86, 105–8
17:4–5	107, 107n31, 108
17:5	107
17:6	108
17:9–10	80, 81, 105
17:18	107, 108
18:10–21	107, 108
18:11–13	88
18:23	110
19	135, 136
19:1–8	95
19:11–21	134
19:12–21	110
19:15	33
19:17–21	134–36
19:19–20	134
19:19–21	110, 112
19:20	84, 110, 135
20	3, 4, 5, 9, 10n36, 11, 109
20:1	110
20:1–3	109
20:1–10	96, 114
20:2–3	138
20:3	113

Scripture Index

(Revelation continued)
Reference	Pages
20:4	84, 112
20:4–5	112
20:4–6	8, 111–12
20:5–6	8
20:7	132
20:7–8	112
20:7–9	113
20:7–10	112–13, 132–34, 134n21
20:7–15	54, 133
20:8	133
20:9	112
20:10	111, 113, 135
20:11–15	112
20:11ff	113n54
22:6	83, 100, 101, 120
22:7	83, 101, 120
22:8	77
22:10	100, 101, 120
22:12	83, 101, 120
22:20	83, 101, 120

EARLY CHRISTIAN WRITINGS

Augustine of Hippo
4, 6, 10n36, 12, 15, 64, 64n37

The City of God

	5
20.6	5n16

Clement of Alexandria
6

Didache
77n3

Dionysius
6

Eusebius

Church History

3.39.7	79n11
3.7	69n11

Hippolytus
25, 78

Irenaeus
6, 25, 78

Jerome
15

Joachim of Fiore
24n48

John Mark
78

Justin Martyr
6, 78

Origen
6, 78

Contra Celsum

2.13	69n11

Papias of Hierapolis
78

GREEK AND ROMAN LITERATURE

Dio Cassius

81

Roman History

5   81n25

Pliny the Elder

91

Natural History

2.86   92n71
17.10   62n29

Strabo

92

Geography

13.4.10   92n72
14.1.37   90n62

Suetonius

81, 84

Twelve Caesars

16	84n41, 125n43
26	84n41, 125n43
28–29	84n41, 125n43
33–35	84n41, 125n43
76	81n24

Tacitus

Annals

4.30	89n58
4.55–56	90n63
12	68n3

Histories

5.8—5.12?   108n36

Tertullian

78

www.ingramcontent.com/pod-product-compliance
Lightning Source LLC
Chambersburg PA
CBHW050817160426
43192CB00010B/1799